Radical Hope

RADICAL
HOPE

EDUCATION AND EQUALITY IN AUSTRALIA

NOEL
PEARSON

Published by Black Inc.,
an imprint of Schwartz Media Pty Ltd
37–39 Langridge Street
Collingwood VIC 3066 Australia
email: enquiries@blackincbooks.com
http://www.blackincbooks.com

The National Library of Australia Cataloguing-in-Publication entry:

Pearson, Noel, 1965-

Radical hope : education and equality in Australia / Noel Pearson.

ISBN: 9781863955300 (pbk.)

Aboriginal Australians--Education.
Education--Government policy--Australia.
Aboriginal Australians--Government policy.

370.994

Printed in Australia by Griffin Press an Accredited ISO AS/ NZS 14001:2004
Environmental Management System printer.

The paper this book is printed on is certified against the
Forest Stewardship Council® Standards. Griffin Press holds
FSC chain of custody certification SGS-COC-005088. FSC
promotes environmentally responsible, socially beneficial and
economically viable management of the world's forests.

FSC
www.fsc.org
MIX
Paper from
responsible sources
FSC® C009448

Contents

RADICAL HOPE

PROLOGUE

For what may we hope? Kant put this question in the first-person singular along with two others – What can I know? and What ought I do? – that he thought essentially marked the human condition. With two centuries of philosophical reflection, it seems that these questions are best transposed to the first-person plural. And with that same hindsight: rather than attempt an *a priori* inquiry, I would like to consider hope as it might arise at one of the limits of human existence ... [Crow Indian Chief] Plenty Coups responded to the collapse of his civilisation with radical hope. What makes this hope *radical* is that it is directed toward a future goodness that transcends the current ability to understand what it is. Radical hope anticipates a good for which those who have the hope as yet lack the appropriate concepts with which to understand it. What would it be for such hope to be justified?

—JONATHAN LEAR, *Radical Hope:*
Ethics in the Face of Cultural Devastation (2006)

Some kind person, I don't know who, sent me a copy of Jonathan Lear's *Radical Hope,* and ever since I read it, this beautiful book has drifted in and out of my thoughts. Professor

Lear is in the Department of Philosophy at the University of Chicago and has a dual interest in philosophy (Aristotle) and psychoanalysis (he was among the few in the late twentieth century prepared to make the case in defence of Freud's legacy against the posthumous lynch mob).

Lear's subject is the last great chief of the Native American Crow Nation, Chief Plenty Coups (1848–1932). Plenty Coups presided over that period of Crow history when the foundations of their classical culture were devastated and the Crow took up a sedentary life on reservation lands in Montana, lands which their chief had fought hard to maintain as the basis for a new life. Plenty Coups led the Crow people through one of those great doors separating entire epochs in human history: from the semi-nomadic life of the warrior-hunter to the domiciled life of an agriculturalist on a government-designated reservation. It is the inexorability of the devastation of the classical culture – foreseen by Plenty Coups in a dream vision – and the loss of it that is the most sorrowful part of the transition, not so much the violence. Violence was part of the old classical paradigm, inseparable from that apex of Crow self-actualisation, individual courage and extreme bravery. But the Crow had lost a way of life, one that the Crow and their neighbouring existential antagonists (the Sioux, the Cheyenne, the Blackfeet and the Arapaho) had regarded as good from time immemorial.

Few epochs come to an end so suddenly without the people of the former epoch being utterly crushed in the course of change to the new order. Yet Chief Plenty Coups led his people through the door to an unknowable future, and he stood his people on their feet to contend with the new world.

Lear's book is an act of ethical re-imagination of the questions confronting Plenty Coups in the most dire period of the history of the Crow Nation: the period when they would lose their old way of life, and stood at risk of losing themselves in the process. Lear's philosophical reconstruction is based on the relevant ethno-historiography pertaining to the Crow, but the original provocation came from Plenty Coups' account of his life, as given to a white man named Frank B. Linderman. The account dealt exclusively with Plenty Coups' childhood and youth, and his exploits as a warrior and hunter in the period before the Crow settled on the reservation. He refused to talk about life after the time of his people's move. Linderman's account of this refusal in an author's note at the end of his book haunted Lear:

> Plenty Coups refused to speak of his life after the passing of the buffalo, so that his story seems to have been broken off, leaving many years unaccounted for. "I have not told you half of what happened when I was young," he said, when urged to go on. "I can think back and tell you much more of war and horse-stealing. But when the buffalo went away the hearts of my people fell to the ground, and they could not lift them up again. After this nothing happened. There was little singing anywhere. Besides," he added sorrowfully, "you know that part of my life as well as I do. You saw what happened to us when the buffalo went away."

It is not my desire here to reduce Lear's project to a crude précis: it is best read in its own right. However, the death and resurrection of Crow ontology is the essence of Lear's thesis about Plenty Coups' courage when he led his people through a Valley of their own Shadow of Death.

In this connexion, the anthropologist W.E.H. Stanner's 1959 essay "Durmugam: A Nangiomeri" comes to mind. Stanner first encountered this man from the Daly River in northern Australia in 1932 in the midst of a large spear fight involving a hundred men and as many supporters and seconds. Stanner's vivid account of this event is superlative, but his description of his first sighting of Durmugam is like walking into the Galleria dell'Accademia and seeing Michelangelo's David sprung to obsidian life:

> In trying to sort out the encounters of pairs, my eyes were drawn and held by an Aboriginal of striking physique and superb carriage who always seemed pinned by an unremitting attack. He seemed, as far as any individual could, to dominate the battlefield. He was so tall that he stood half a head above the tallest there. His muscular power was apparent in his bulk but it was the grace and intensity of his fighting which captured my attention. His favourite posture was to fling arms and legs as wide as possible as though to make himself the maximum target. Having drawn and evaded a spear he would often counter with a dexterity and speed remarkable in so large a man. His fluent movements in avoiding injury – an inclination of the head, a sway of the body, the lifting of an arm or a leg,

a half turn – always seemed minimal. I saw his spears strike home several times. As they did, the roars of exultation from his own side, and of rage from the other, would bring a rally to both. He himself stayed unwounded through the afternoon after a peerless display of skill and courage.

The battle died, as if by agreement, towards sundown and some of the antagonists began to fraternise, others to drift away. No one had been mortally hurt though many had painful flesh-wounds. There was some talk of continuing the fight another day. As I moved about making my enquiries, the tall Aboriginal came smilingly across and asked me in a civil way if I had liked the fight. I asked who he was and he told me that he was Durmugam, a Nangiomeri, and that Europeans called him Smiler. I then realised that here was the man widely believed by Europeans to be the most murderous black in the region.

His appearance at this moment was truly formidable. The glaring ochre, the tousled hair above the pipe-clayed forehead band, the spears, and something opaque in his eyes made him seem the savage incarnate. He stood at least 6 feet 3 inches, and must have weighed a sinewy 180 pounds. But his voice was musical, his manner easy, and his smile disarming. I was much taken with him. I noticed particularly how smoothly contoured was his body, how small his feet, how sensitive and finely boned his hands. Other men present were more heavily muscled but none had so large and so finely moulded a physique. His carriage was perfect, and he walked very erect, with head held high, and with quick, purposeful steps. Yet there was nothing truculent or overbearing about him.

Stanner traces his association with the man who would from then on become his new main informant ("always one of the most exciting moments of fieldwork") to their last meeting in 1958, when the old man, now grey and with failing sight ("but still erect, and still a striking figure of a man"), was consumed with troubles – a year before his passing. Durmugam comes to mind because he is one of the recorded historical figures caught in these vital phases of history: the time of the collapse of the old and the onset of the new. A man with sharp hopes shared by his fellows ("the vital will of the blacks to make something of the ruined life around them") – except that in this case Durmugam's hopes would be unrealised.

Durmugam was born in the second decade of European and Chinese penetration into the Daly River, when the tribes of the region were already in a parlous state from disease, grog, opium, inter-tribal fighting and violence at the hands of miners and farmers ("He remembers only two things clearly of his earliest days on the Daly, where his mother died at the copper mine – endless bloody fights between the river and the back-country tribes, and numbers of drink-sodden Aborigines lying out in the rain"). There was heavy depopulation of the area ("any anthropologist would find indirect genealogical proof that scores, if not hundreds, of Aborigines must have died. Many from unrecorded causes").

The High Culture of the Nangiomeri was on the ropes, and Durmugam, having been brought up by his mother's brother, was bitter that he had not been told anything of the secret male culture of his tribe, as would have been the normal course of things in an earlier time ("He had to learn this as a man from other tribes which shared it, or had known of it, and he felt there was some element of shame in such a thing").

As a young man he was initiated into the High Culture that was still vital on the distant Victoria River ("He was given his first bullroarers. He began to learn too of the lost secret life of the Nangiomeri") and this became the defining object of his life ("As he told me of these experiences, in the sequence of his life-story, it was as though his mind and heart had suddenly unified").

While the High Culture of the Victoria River mob remained strong, the first phase of contact had ruptured and reduced the High Culture on the Daly:

> Many of the preconditions of the traditional culture were gone – a sufficient population, a self-sustaining economy, a discipline by elders, a confident dependency on nature – and, with the preconditions, went much of the culture, including its secret male rites. What was left of the tradition amounted to a Low Culture – some secular ceremonies, magical practices, mundane institutions and rules-of-thumb for a prosaic life.

Stanner describes the revival of what he called a new High Culture in the 1920s, through the emergence of a cult of which Durmugam and other young men were adherents

("It is clear these young men were fired, and also felt under some command. Durmugam was one of a group of three who seem to have set about remodelling their lives and their culture"). When Stanner first visited the river in the 1930s, the cult was spreading ("I should think that no scrap of European prestige remained. I found an unshaken belief that Aboriginal ways were right, even at the level of the Low Culture").

But by the time Stanner returned in 1952, following a long absence after 1935, he found Durmugam an aged man and he and his fellows' dreams of maintaining their High Culture had turned to dust ("I had the impression that the traditional culture was on its last legs … the High Culture had not prospered; many of the young men openly derided the secret life"). His subsequent visits during the 1950s found Durmugam in steadily worsening mood ("I noted too, for the first time, an element of desperation and pessimism for the future. At the same time, there were signs of antipathy in him towards Europeanism and a deepening attachment to the old Aboriginal ways").

It was the breakdown of the old law that confounded Durmugam and gave rise to his problems:

> He was filled with angry contempt for the young men of the day. "They can throw a spear," he said, "but can they *make* one? Can they find their own food in the bush?" He told me of a conversation with one youth who was deriding the bullroarer. Durmugam told him that it might cost him his life. The youth said, with a shrug, "If I live, I live; if I die, I die." I asked Durmugam what he said

then. Durmugam said: "Well, fuck you." The use of English for expression in such crises had become common in the area. It was a means of appeal to a wider world, a new code, and a new scale of values.

Stanner's last visit in 1958 saw the old man in deep troubles. His favourite wife had run off with the son of his first wife ("a great humiliation to a man still alive"). A married daughter had been abducted by a youth whom Durmugam had long befriended and he had lost contact with his granddaughter ("the apple of Durmugam's eye"). Another wife had been sexually assaulted by a number of men ("on the ground that she had illicitly seen a bullroarer in Durmugam's camp – a pretext, he said vehemently, a lie. Would he, who knew the dangers, be likely to have a bullroarer there? They were all hidden in the bush").

He was unable to resort to justice under Aboriginal law for these grievances, yet none of his appeals to the authorities could right these wrongs for him either ("The young men were 'flash' (out of hand, conceited), not listening to anyone, not caring for anything. Much trouble would come from this, trouble for everyone. He grieved over the unfilial conduct of his son. Who ever heard of a son running away with his mother? Who ever heard of a son helping another man to abduct a married sister?").

In discussing the wider context of the official policy of assimilation, Stanner notes that the old contempt of previous generations of white Australians for Aboriginal people had by this time receded in favour of a new solicitude which

animated the new policy, and he pinpoints the locus of
Durmugam's crisis:

> But old contempt and new solicitude have a common
> element: a kind of sightlessness towards the central prob-
> lems of what it is to be a blackfellow in the here-and-now
> of Australian life. For this reason hundreds of natives
> have gone through, and will go through, the torment of
> powerlessness which Durmugam suffered.

Durmugam passed into a new epoch whose defining condition was the torment of powerlessness. Stanner observes:

> The secularisation was far-reaching and corrosive, psychi-
> cally and socially. The young man's remark, "If I live, I
> live; if I die, I die", had seemed to Durmugam monstrous.
> To him, *how* a man lived and what he lived *for* were of
> first importance. But he himself had in part succumbed.
> He now spent much time playing poker for money (there
> were five aces in one of his packs of cards); and, for the
> first time in his life, he accepted money from me. His
> material wants were more complex and at a higher level.
> He still went bootless, but wore a hat and well-kept shirt
> and trousers.

How a man lived and what he lived for were of first importance.
The discussion that I would now like to have (and which I
believe is vital to Aboriginal people) is concerned with what
it might mean to be a serious person and what it might mean

to be a serious people. One answer to Jonathan Lear's question, "What would it be for such [radical] hope to be justified?" is that those who harbour, hold and project such hope must be serious. Hope founded on mere optimism is not serious, and a serious person is not readily gulled into hope, especially not by his or her own wishful thinking. A serious person or people are only limited by whatever fund of determination they have built up and consolidated over time. When one struggles against all odds, determination alone is no guarantee of success, but you won't get very far without it. And sometimes it will seem as though determination is all that one has. Part of the quality of seriousness is determination. Another part is discipline.

serious

Out of the rites of the classical High Culture emerged serious Aborigines. It is a seriousness akin to that of which St Paul wrote, in his first letter to the Corinthians: "When I was a child, I spake as a child, I understood as a child, I thought as a child: but when I became a man, I put away childish things. For now we see through a glass, darkly; but then face to face: now I know in part; but then shall I know even as also I am known."

The great vulnerability of Aboriginal people is that the institutions of our culture that mandated seriousness fell apart and have been only partially and inadequately replaced or rejuvenated. It is these most vital institutions which Durmugam and his fellows were anxious to maintain, but were, alas, unable to. Midst the ruins of their old world and the mutations of the new, they were seeking an accommodation of those things that made Aborigines a serious people.

I postulate that all pre-modern peoples carried within their cultures some institutional essence of what made and maintained them as peoples. Some things that prescribed how they should live and what were their sustaining ideals as a people. By contrast, modern peoples, secular and unanchored, come to feel the double-edged sword of freedom from traditional orthodoxy: this includes the freedom to lose one's identity and to assimilate into a dominant culture. Yet those who resist assimilation have no protection against its inexorable advance if they have lost the things that made them a serious people.

There are two circumstances in which people need to be serious in order to have any chance.

First, when people live in hard places. The harder the place, the more serious must be the people. Human societies that occupy some of the hardest, most inhospitable – most economically irrational – places on Earth require severely serious people to sustain such places as homes. Strong rationales are needed to maintain the hearth in hard places.

Secondly, when people are striving to maintain and to transmit to future generations their pre-modern cultures and languages in a modern, global world. The more esoteric and the less economically relevant these cultures and languages are to the imperatives of the modern, global world, the more serious the people must be in order to retain their own culture and language.

My notion of seriousness is about orthodoxy. A serious person, in the sense that I am concerned with here, is an orthodox person.

Facing the abyss, many Aborigines could only do one thing to keep the flame alive: preserve their knowledge through ethnographic recordings for what was often some as yet unclear and unknown application that future generations may make of them. To pass something on to the other side. The anthropologist Peter Sutton once spoke of the zeal with which the Flinders Islands–Cape Melville man Johnny Flinders, with whom he had worked in the 1970s, engaged in recording knowledge of his language and culture:

> Among old people like Johnny Flinders there was a really strong feeling based on the knowledge that they were in fact the last ones who grew up in the bush and knew the country in detail. There was a very strong desire to record these things. Johnny would often say, "You got another book here? We gotta fill up another book. Fill up another notebook." He was keen to leave what he knew for others.

"fill up another book"

As with Durmugam, the secret to serious peoplehood was not something that could be transmitted in living form, merely perhaps preserved. Not only because the High Culture paradigm had collapsed, but because even where it did not and has not, there is a fatal flaw in the way in which Aboriginal Law has dealt with the European vices. These vices being unprecedented, Aboriginal Law did not evolve to proscribe these vices according to comparable principles of precedent. In Durmugam's case, Stanner records that in his last years, the serious man had capitulated to one such vice: gambling on poker for money.

The whole point about orthodoxy is that such vices are anathema to it. There is little to wonder about why Jewish, Islamic and other forms of cultural and religious orthodoxy spurn alcohol. And yet the Aboriginal High Culture that has survived to the present is fatally compromised by the assumption that the Law which underpins this High Culture does not have anything to say about the European vices. What started as bewilderment turned into a disastrous precedent of omission. The contradictions of that unnatural alliance between black conservatives and white libertarians play no small role in this tragedy of denial over the most recent decades. No serious people can emerge from ancient rites which offer no prescriptions in respect of things that are fundamentally destructive of the very things that are supposed to be the purpose of the rites: the continuity of the culture and the people.

It is time to ask: are we Aborigines a serious people? Do we have serious leaders? Do we have the seriousness necessary to maintain the hard places we call home? Do we have the seriousness necessary to maintain our languages, traditions and knowledge?

I strive to avoid wishful thinking but one can never be immune from it. The truth is that I am prone to bouts of doubt and sadness around these questions. But I have hope. Our hope is dependent upon education. Our hope depends on how serious we become about the education of our people.

EVEN KEELING, NO EXCUSES

We've got to say to our children, yes, if you're African-American, the odds of growing up amid crime and gangs are higher. Yes, if you live in a poor neighbourhood, you will face challenges that somebody in a wealthy suburb does not have to face. But that's not a reason to get bad grades. That's not a reason to cut class. That's not a reason to give up on your education and drop out of school. No one has written your destiny for you. Your destiny is in your hands. You cannot forget that. That's what we have to teach all of our children. No excuses. No excuses.

You get that education, all those hardships will just make you stronger, better able to compete. Yes we can.

To parents – to parents, we can't tell our kids to do well in school and then fail to support them when they get home. You can't just contract out parenting. For our kids to excel, we have to accept our responsibility to help them learn. That means putting away the Xbox. Putting our kids to bed at a reasonable hour. It means attending those parent–teacher conferences and reading to our children and helping them with their homework.

And by the way, it means we need to be there for our neighbours' sons and daughters. We need to go back to

the time, back to the day when we parents saw somebody, saw some kid fooling around and – it wasn't your
child, but they'll whup you anyway. Or at least they'll tell
your parents. That's the meaning of community. That's
how we can reclaim the strength and the determination
and the hopefulness that helped us come so far; helped
us make a way out of no way.

It also means pushing our children to set their sights a
little bit higher. They might think they've got a pretty
good jump shot or a pretty good flow, but our kids can't
all aspire to be LeBron or Lil Wayne. I want them aspiring to be scientists and engineers, doctors and teachers,
not just ballers and rappers. I want them aspiring to be a
Supreme Court Justice. I want them aspiring to be the
President of the United States of America.

—BARACK OBAMA, 17 July 2009

Ships of change and evolution, progress and regress, chart
their course through history with the winds and currents of
political economy buffeting them from all sides. It is in the
nature of these forces that such ships never sail evenly on
their keel. The ships lean – indeed are pushed – in accord
with the prevailing winds and the forces of the sea, either
portside or starboard. Only in those unlikely times when the
wind is directly behind them will they sail even. Those who
would captain ships of sail cannot avoid their vessel turning
on an uneven keel.

On 17 July 2009, on the one-hundredth anniversary of
the founding of the National Association for the Advance-

ment of Colored People, President Barack Obama delivered a precisely balanced speech on the subject of the history and future of African-Americans in the United States. That half of his speech which dealt with education and personal responsibility – the No Excuses part – resounded throughout the country, and indeed the world. The other half, dealing with structural barriers and historical legacy, was not exactly ignored, but it was the exhortation of black parents and their children that captured public attention.

The ship's captain was reportedly miffed about the unbalanced reporting of his balanced speech. "I've noticed that when I talk about personal responsibility in the African-American community, that gets highlighted," Obama said in an Oval Office interview with the *Washington Post*'s Eugene Robinson a day later. "But then the whole other half of the speech, where I talked about government's responsibility … that somehow doesn't make news."

Whether Obama truly believes that one's most assiduous attempts at intellectually balanced analysis can be expected to play out in the turbulence of the real world in the way one intends is not clear to me. Whether the president felt it necessary when talking to a brother from the *Washington Post* to try and right the ship for the benefit of his black audience, or whether he truly believes that a perfect equilibrium between structure and behaviour can be achieved through calibrated leadership – that too is not clear.

The Harvard lawyer in Obama has developed the rhetorical means to navigate a perfectly nuanced third way through a conflict. Only the former president Bill Clinton could give him a run for his money when it comes to this penetrating ability. Yet whereas my sense is that Clinton (through cynicism if nothing else) understood the difference between rhetorical figure and reality, I don't know whether Obama expects to be taken exactly at his word.

In any case, his complaint to the black community about the unbalanced reporting of his speech worked to preserve the president's credentials in the eyes of another brother writing in the *New York Times*. Brent Staples wrote on 23 July:

> Successful African-Americans ... are often employed as weapons in the age-old campaign to discredit, and even demean, the disadvantaged.
>
> Mr Obama has refused to play this role, even though people have tried to thrust it upon him.
>
> Up to now, he has been consistently and wrongly portrayed as a stern black exceptionalist who takes Negroes to task for not meeting his standard.
>
> He suggested that the news media had overemphasized his remarks about "personal responsibility" – a venerable theme in the African-American church – while disregarding "the whole other half of the speech", which included a classic exercise in civil-rights oratory.
>
> People who have heretofore viewed Mr Obama as a "post-racial" abstraction were no doubt surprised by [his remarks on the arrest of Harvard African-American scholar Henry Louis Gates Jr]. This could be because they were hearing him fully for the first time.

I wrote in the *Monthly* in 2008 that while most people accept that human prospects are affected by both socio-economic structure and individual behaviour, they generally fall on one or other side of this fine line in attributing responsibility. Obama, I claimed, is on balance a structural thinker and much concerned with the legacy of oppression.

Indeed, the "whole other half of the speech" laid out a conventional progressive account of the structural factors underpinning black disadvantage (what Staples described as "a classic exercise in civil-rights oratory"):

> And yet, even as we celebrate the remarkable achievements of the past 100 years ... we know that too many barriers still remain.
>
> ... [Make] no mistake: The pain of discrimination is still felt in America ... But we also know that prejudice and discrimination – at least the most blatant types of prejudice and discrimination – are not even the steepest barriers to opportunity today. The most difficult barriers include structural inequalities that our nation's legacy of discrimination has left behind; inequalities still plaguing too many communities and too often the object of national neglect ... I remember visiting a Chicago school in a rough neighborhood when I was a community organizer, and some of the children gathered round me. And I remember thinking how remarkable it was that all of these children seemed so full of hope, despite being born into poverty, despite being delivered, in some cases, into addiction, despite all the obstacles they were already

facing – you could see that spark in their eyes. They were the equal of children anywhere.

And I remember the principal of the school telling me that soon that sparkle would begin to dim, that things would begin to change; that soon, the laughter in their eyes would begin to fade; that soon, something would shut off inside, as it sunk in – because kids are smarter than we give them credit for – as it sunk in that their hopes would not come to pass. Not because they weren't smart enough, not because they weren't talented enough, not because of anything about them inherently, but because, by accident of birth, they had not received a fair chance in life.

It was inevitable that the headline message from the president's address would be "No Excuses." No Excuses has been growing as an educational movement in the United States over the past two decades, in concert with the burgeoning charter-school movement. It is premised on the idea that the achievement gap can be closed between students of different racial groups in the United States if you get schooling right – and that the socio-economic and racial backgrounds of students are no reason for under-achievement.

In Australia the under-achievement of disadvantaged students and disadvantaged schools has been an intractable problem for just as long as it has been considered unacceptable. Ubiquitous, it has long been the subject of governmental reform commitments – many of the "No child will live in poverty by 2000" variety – which have had little or no effect.

The Indigenous Australian education disaster is a subset of a wider problem: a persistent failure to close the achievement gap between disadvantaged students and disadvantaged schools on the one hand and the wider school population on the other.

There is a fundamental issue here: can educational disadvantage be overcome without overcoming broader socio-economic disadvantage? In other words, will there be educational disadvantage for as long as there is broader social and economic inequality?

It is too early to give up on the classical ideal that educational improvement can take place despite socio-economic disadvantage. We do not have to fix all social and economic problems to close the achievement gap. Indeed, the opposite is true: educational progress is an antecedent condition to overcoming broader social and economic disadvantage.

But where in the world is the classical ideal proven in practice?

It has ever been the case that individual students from disadvantaged backgrounds overcome social and economic disadvantage and succeed. The problem we are dealing with here is a social one. The onus falls on those of us who believe in the classical ideal to show that educational reform can produce broad-based social transformation among disadvantaged students, and not just the raising up of the few.

No Excuses

In recent times, the United States has seen a kind of insurgency movement in educational reform, one that has taken many forms. Models that give grounds for optimism come from the best of the American charter-school movement as well as from some stand-out public schools.

Charter schools are publicly funded and have been granted independence from the constraints of the public system of the American state in which they operate, while being held accountable for achieving commitments set out in the school's charter. Starting with Minnesota in 1991, forty states in the United States now have legislation governing the establishment, funding and accountability of charter schools. While there are today over 4000 such schools in America, they represent a small fraction of the total number of publicly funded schools in that country.

Two broad conclusions can be reached about charter schools. First, there have been failures as well as successes. One estimate is that of the 4000 schools that were spawned, only 25 per cent of them are any good. Clearly there are lessons to be learned from the experience of opening up school provision to enthusiasts at large. The risk of Boy's and Girl's Own Adventures in Schooling ending in tears is real.

But the second conclusion is that a significant minority of these charter schools have succeeded in closing the achievement gap for racially and socially disadvantaged students. The most successful of these schools have now been scaled up to franchises, spread out across the United States.

When searching for the provenance of the No Excuses educational insurgency, one cannot go past the precocious founder (she was twenty-one when she began her crusade) of Teach For America, the Princeton graduate Wendy Kopp.

Enticing high-achieving graduates from Ivy League universities to devote two years to teaching in disadvantaged schools after a short period of training (and with ongoing support), Kopp's TFA has recruited more than 14,000 graduates to its corps since 1990. Working in parallel with the charter-school movement across the various states, Kopp's theory of change – based on the idea that a certain proportion of these high-achievers would stay in education, and, just as importantly, that TFA alumni would go on to become education-reform advocates in whatever fields they ended up in – has yielded some critical results.

One such alumnus, the chancellor of the Columbia school district in Washington, D.C., Michelle Rhee (who, together with the New York education tsar Joel Klein, is Julia Gillard's source of inspiration for education reform), went on to found an offshoot, The New Teacher Project, following her stint with Teach For America. This project has also now recruited more than 10,000 high-achieving career-changers from other professions into teaching.

Two other renowned TFA alumni are the founders of the Knowledge Is Power Program (KIPP) charter-school franchise, Mike Feinberg and Dave Levin, who founded their first middle school in Houston, Texas, in 1994 and now have eighty-two schools across nineteen states.

"Work Hard. Be Nice" is the motto of the Knowledge Is Power network. KIPP aims to send all of its students to college: classrooms are even named after colleges and universities which students aspire to attend. Bill Gates recently described its singular approach to teaching:

Now there are a few places, very few, where great teachers are being made. A good example of one is a set of charter schools called KIPP … They take the poorest kids and over 96 per cent of their high-school graduates go to four-year colleges. And the whole spirit and attitude in those schools is very different than in the normal public school. They're team teaching, they're constantly improving their teachers, they're taking data, the test scores, and saying to a teacher, "Hey, you've caused this amount of increase," and so they're deeply engaged in making teaching better.

When you actually go and sit in one of these class-rooms, at first it's very bizarre. I sat down and I thought, what is going on? The teacher was running around, the energy level was high, they're having a sports rally or something. What's going on? And the teacher was con-stantly scanning to see which kids weren't paying atten-tion, which kids were bored, and calling on kids, rapidly, putting things up on the board. It was a very dynamic environment because particularly in those middle-school years, fifth to eighth grade, keeping people engaged and setting the tone that everybody in the classroom needs to pay attention – nobody gets to make fun of it or have the position of the kid who doesn't want to be there, every-body needs to be involved.

I will consider KIPP's approach to effective teaching later in this essay.

Knowledge Is Power is the best known of the charter-school franchises, but there are other standout examples. Some operate with additional funding from philanthropic and corporate sponsors, while others have the explicit aim of demonstrating that educational reform can be achieved at equivalent funding levels to public schools. Many charter schools are new start-ups. The various franchises are distinct, and they adopt different educational philosophies and practices.

There are also instances of public schools in the United States that have solved seemingly intractable problems of under-achievement while remaining within the public school system. The Gering public school district in Nebraska has a large proportion of students from Hispanic backgrounds. Of twenty-five school districts in that state, Gering had the worst literacy test scores in 2004 but the seventh-highest by 2008. This dramatic improvement – particularly among Hispanic students – was driven by district-wide reform of literacy instruction.

The common feature of all these different schools is that the socio-economic background and personal circumstances of their disadvantaged students cannot be put forward as a reason for under-achievement. This applies not only to students and parents, but also to education providers – the franchise, the school, the school leader and the teachers.

No Excuses has its origins here. Steven Wilson, the chief of the Ascend Charter School in New York, gives the following definition:

Highly educated, driven, and generally young teachers lead their students in a rigorous academic program, tightly aligned with state standards, that aims to set every child on the path to college. The approach has been dubbed "No Excuses" schooling because founders and staff steadfastly reject explanations from any quarter for low achievement, whether district apologists' appeal to demographic destiny or a child's excuse for failing to complete an assignment.

This school of thought should not be pigeonholed to the political Right or the Left.

In Cape York Peninsula, we embraced No Excuses and, inspired by Abigail and Stephan Thernstrom's 2003 book *No Excuses: Closing the Racial Gap in Learning*, hammered out the following nostrums to guide our approach to education reform:

- Indigenous Australian culture is a culture of responsibility and reciprocity. Ours is a culture of law and learning. Ours is a culture of transmission of knowledge. Our culture is our strength.
- We will take our responsibilities to our children. We will not allow other people to use the fact that our children are Indigenous as an excuse for educational failure.
- Our children have their own culture and languages, other children have other cultures and languages. No culture or language predisposes children for educational failure.
- The fact that some of our children come from disadvantaged, and even dysfunctional, backgrounds, will no longer be an excuse for educational failure.

- We will understand and be sensitive to the difficulties facing our children and we are going to find every support to deal with them, but we will not allow these difficulties to be an excuse for educational failure.
- It will not be an excuse for the children.
- It will not be an excuse for the parents or community.
- It will not be an excuse for the principal and the teachers.
- It will not be an excuse for the education system and all of us who say we are committed to Indigenous education reform.

I came to understand that the most important target audience for the No Excuses approach is educators. While some parents and community members will resort to excuse-making, the parties most susceptible to this are the principals, teachers and education-department bureaucrats who use student background – the dysfunctional circumstances of their lower-class students – as an alibi for schooling failure.

[handwritten margin note: educators are excuse makers]

In Australia, there seems to be a contradiction at the heart of our commitment to public education. On the one hand, educators are briefed with the task of enabling disadvantaged students to transcend their background: to defy the social and economic forces of class predestination. On the other hand, the same educators (and the society that gives them their brief) are likely to believe that educational inequality will always reflect social and economic inequality: that the further down the ladder you go, the less prospect there is of encountering a school of willing students and able teachers.

Is this just the difference between opportunity and outcome? That is, does it reflect a belief that our commitment to public education can only guarantee universal opportunity, but not universal outcomes? On this view, a minority of the exceptional children from disadvantaged backgrounds will be able to capitalise on the opportunity – but the overall social result will be the reproduction of disadvantage.

Is the hope for social transformation through tackling disadvantage via public education just a recurrent cycle of hope triumphing over experience? We know we're not going to get very far, but we can't not try (so we set out great ambitions and gee ourselves up for the challenge).

Even as I write these thoughts, they send me down that depressing curve of the would-be reformer's post-adrenal reality check: what if the gravity of social and economic inequality is as inescapable as Jupiter's? What if no education reform can be launched out of such an environment?

We must seriously consider the case against No Excuses.

Richard Rothstein is a leading critic of the claims of the No Excuses movement in general, and the KIPP charter schools in particular. In his 2004 book *Class and Schools: Using Social, Economic and Educational Reform to Close the Black–White Achievement Gap*, he firstly points out that KIPP can only be a boutique operation because it is creaming the teacher pool: the approach requires the highest-achieving teachers. Even if new high-achievers are recruited to teaching, the average school will never have teachers as able as the ones KIPP recruits. Rothstein's point is confirmed in a 2008 analysis by the leading charter-school advocate Steven Wilson. So the question remains: KIPP may be a proven boutique, but is it scaleable? There are now a little over eighty KIPP schools and perhaps 1000 good charter schools across the United States. But there are more than 80,000 public schools – most of them larger than the average charter school.

Rothstein's second argument is that KIPP's students are not representative of student populations in disadvantaged neighbourhoods. In effect KIPP schools are taking the cream of the ghettos. KIPP leaders resist this charge: statistics show that KIPP students are only somewhat less disadvantaged economically than students in comparable regular public schools, and that literacy levels among incoming KIPP students are close to those of regular public-school students. And in any case, KIPP seeks to insure against selectivity by offering student places by lottery.

Rothstein further argues that the parents of KIPP students are more motivated than typical parents of disadvantaged children. It is true that parents make an active choice to enrol their children in KIPP schools. However, KIPP students are on average significantly behind their peers before they start in KIPP schools. Their results generally improve significantly only after enrolment. It appears likely that the school makes the difference, because typical parents of KIPP students are obviously not able to make any major contribution to their children's academic development, and KIPP itself does not expect this.

At a more fundamental level, Rothstein questions whether school reform can indeed close the larger part of the educational gap, even if it were possible to provide all disadvantaged students with education of the same standard as in KIPP schools. He contends that "The influence of social class is probably so powerful that schools cannot overcome it, no matter how well trained are their teachers and no matter how well designed are their instructional programs and climates."

Rothstein points to the sheer improbability of the claim that the accumulated burden of early-onset disadvantage – from genetic via prenatal to early childhood factors – can be significantly made up for at school. For example, the differences between children of different social classes in the size of their vocabularies and other variables of language development are very large by the time children begin kindergarten.

Professor Walter Benn Michaels has taken the argument of the determinative power of social class even further in his provocative book *The Trouble with Diversity: How We Learned To Love Identity and Ignore Inequality*. Michaels argues that policies for diversity – racial, gender, cultural or otherwise – serve to hide the fact that class differences by and large reproduce themselves through the education system.

Family wealth, according to Michaels, is overwhelmingly the main determinant of educational achievement from early childhood to university. Since the entire school system is structured to enable the rich to out-compete the poor, the proposed solutions to the exclusion of poor people (including various kinds of financial assistance) are irrelevant when students from lower social strata cannot get into the prestigious universities:

As long as the elite schools are themselves open to any-body who's smart enough and/or hardworking enough to get into them, we see no injustice in reaping the benefits. It's okay if schools are technologies for reproducing in-equality as long as they are also technologies for justify-ing it. But the justification will only work if … there really are rich people and poor people at Harvard. If there really aren't – if it's your wealth (or your family's wealth) that makes it possible for you to go to the elite school in the first place – then, of course, the real source of your success is not the fact that you went to an elite school but the fact that your parents were rich enough to give you the back-ground and preparation that got you admitted to the elite school.

In the debate between advocates of No Excuses and the proponents of structural explanations for the achievement gap, Barack Obama seems anxious not to alienate either side. Obama obviously believes education to be the great trans-former, the means of social and economic uplift. But, on the other hand, Obama does not seem fully to believe in the power of education to overcome the structural barriers an African-American will encounter from childhood to adulthood.

I have never disputed that structural barriers hold disad-vantaged groups back. In my monograph *Our Right To Take Responsibility,* published in 2000, I wrote:

> Make no mistake, racism is a terrible burden. It attacks the spirit. It attacks self-esteem and the soul in ways that

those who are not subjected to it would have not an ink-
ling of. Racism is a major handicap: it results in Aboriginal people not having access to opportunities, in not
recognising opportunities when they arise, in not being
able to seize and hold onto opportunities when they recognise them. Australians concerned about the position of
Aboriginal people in this country should not underestimate the decisive role that racism plays in the wellbeing
of Aboriginal individuals and society. Australians need to
stop kidding themselves that "racism isn't all that bad –
black people should just get over it and on with it". If you
are black in this country, you start life with a great and
crushing burden.

And in 2005, explaining the need for reform in Cape York, I
and my colleagues stated that:

> Cape York is operating at a social-order deficit, largely
> due to a breakdown of social norms. We need to be
> clear that this deficit is the legacy of our history, of
> dispossession, trauma, discrimination and the under-
> mining of indigenous leadership and authority. Our
> people have been immensely scarred by this history: it
> was what made us vulnerable to substance abuse in the
> first place.

I would agree with Obama that the deep historical roots of
racism are not a legacy that can easily be overcome.

"Don't underestimate the degree to which a speech like the

one I gave yesterday gets magnified throughout the African-American community," Obama told Eugene Robinson.

Not just blacks in America. Educrats in Australia too. Obama's speech provoked a twittering of emails from bureaucrats in the Indigenous education twitocracy enthusing about how the speech "spoke a lot of home truths about how government action needs to work in tandem with family action to achieve strong outcomes in Indigenous education" and (somewhat ambitiously, I would have thought) even suggesting, "Maybe his speech offers some ideas for the speeches we craft." Speeches, presumably, for the Sir Lesley Pattersons ministering to our state education departments.

It was hard not to notice that the same bureaucrats who broke out in histaminic outrage that we in Cape York were "blaming the victim" when we articulated No Excuses here a few years ago were now reacting rapturously to Obama saying the same thing. No matter that an objective analytical view might counsel Zen-like transcendence, one's viscera are only ever somewhat and only ever sometimes pacified from writhing like a tangle of fitful snakes in a belly of brine.

Unlike Obama, I think it futile to complain. I have never been under any illusion that one actor can advance more than one side in a dialectical tension. There is no even keeling in the real world.

GROUNDHOG DAY

Pretending not to remember was given deep intellectual roots by Descartes. He saw memory as an obstacle, as "weak and unstable." Thought could strengthen it but the answer was to free our intellect by marginalising our memory. And so he conceived that we could will ourselves to forget in order to be free to marshal our arguments for the future. By consigning much of what we remembered to the written page, memory would lose its power over us and we would, more or less, free up space in our minds for independent thought. A *tabula rasa* to achieve individual freedom. I would call this an attempt at thought without context, which presents certain problems.

—JOHN RALSTON SAUL, *On Equilibrium* (2001)

That most policy fails is not much acknowledged in public life. Governments and their bureaucracies – creators, filers and archivists of massive piles of history – strangely have no memory. The only history that is remembered is that which might serve a current purpose: it is as though the rest never happened. Governments and their bureaucracies are informed by everything other than memory of what was done five years ago, ten years ago and eighteen years ago. Politics are remembered, policies are not.

Each new policy paradigm is announced with scarcely any recognition that what is being done today is Mark IV of an approach which has never shown much success, or that it is a 180-degree turnaround from what we were convinced was correct some years back. Sure, there is the usual summary at the start of the policy document that touches on the history of an issue – but this is not memory in its true and useful sense. It is just chronology.

The problem with memory is that it may entail, among other things, doubt, self-awareness and moral responsibility. These are not usual or desired qualities in public administration.

Politicians and bureaucrats and the systems in which they operate have a strong aversion to real memory. This amnesia must serve somebody's interests. Is it the interest in the need to present everything as "new" and "fresh"? Old proposals that might have failed cannot be regurgitated unless they are presented afresh and anew. Is it the abiding interest in not having to confront the failure of past proposals, and to account for them? Is it a desire to forget reality's reproaches to ideology?

The Queensland Labor government under Premier Peter Beattie proposed in 2000 to halve the number of Indigenous people in the state's criminal justice system by 2011. An "Aboriginal Justice Agreement" was solemnly signed between Aboriginal leaders and the premier and senior ministers. A halfway-mark evaluation was conducted which showed the numbers had increased during the first years of the agreement. We are now approaching the target date set by the Justice Agreement, but who will remember the policy when we don't even come close to our goals?

It is arguable that Indigenous affairs are marginal, and therefore vulnerable to this form of vacuous policy-making – that policies relevant to the mainstream are taken more seriously by governments of the day.

From Sunshine State to Not-So-Smart State

Education was arguably the centrepiece policy of the four-term Beattie Labor government in Queensland from 1998 to 2008. Beattie's Big Idea was that Queensland would make an evolutionary leap from the Sunshine State to the Smart State. From a surfer's paradise and regional backwater, Beattie's idea was that Queensland would become a Biotechnology Valley supported by the country's best education system. His successor as premier, Anna Bligh, was minister for education for almost five years while the Smart State was under construction.

At the end of ten years and four terms, three held by very large majorities, what was the result?

At the end of 2008 the Bligh government was thrown into a spin when it was revealed that rather than the Sunshine State becoming the Smart State, we were the Dumb State according to the results of the 2008 National Assessment Program – Literacy and Numeracy and the 2007 Trends in International Mathematics and Science Study. Only the Northern Territory performed worse.

Anna Bligh immediately commissioned a review by the

head of the Australian Council for Educational Research, Geoff Masters. Masters delivered his report in April 2009. I do not intend to traverse the issues in the Masters review, nor his recommendations. I simply note that he confirmed that at the bottom of Queensland's failed education system sit Aboriginal and Torres Strait Islander children:

> Indigenous students in Queensland primary schools, on average, have significantly lower levels of literacy and numeracy than non-indigenous students. Approximately 25 to 35 per cent fail to reach national minimum standards at each of Years 3, 5, 7 and 9 (compared with 5 to 10 per cent of non-indigenous students). Indigenous students in remote parts of the state perform in the bottom 10 per cent of all students nationally; Indigenous students in very remote parts of the state perform in the bottom 5 per cent of all students nationally. By Year 9, the gap between non-indigenous Queensland students and Indigenous students living in very remote parts of the state is, on average, equivalent to six to seven years of school.

The Aboriginal education–achievement gap is a history of failure that has defied reform attempts for decades. There is a predictable cycle of public revelation and consternation about failure followed by a new policy review, a new policy framework and a new commitment. This Groundhog Day occurs every three to five years.

A 2004 report on Indigenous education produced by a committee chaired by Dr Chris Sarra listed a succession of reform initiatives over the past twenty years, stating that "there has been no shortage of advice to government about how to address the imbalance in outcomes between Indigenous and non-Indigenous students." It referred to the Aboriginal Education Policy endorsed by all Australian governments in 1989, which "set out 21 long-term goals with the objective of achieving educational equity for Indigenous Australians by the year 2000." The report went on:

> Other major reports and strategies on Indigenous education have reached similar conclusions about the systemic failure of education systems and the need to take urgent action to improve outcomes for Indigenous students in the interests of communities and the State. For whatever reasons, the exhortations to act and the numerous strategies and government-supported programs have failed to convert the rhetoric into a reality that Indigenous communities can value.

In a 2009 paper for the Centre for Independent Studies, Helen Hughes and Mark Hughes set out a similar catalogue of reform commitments, with particular reference to the goals that currently form part of the Council of Australian Governments' educational targets. With regard to the literacy gap, the authors point out that national targets have shifted from "fix the problem in four years" to "fix half the problem in ten years."

When we in Cape York began our welfare-reform advocacy in 1999, the Beattie government released its new Indigenous education framework, "Partners for Success." Broadly, this framework moved Queensland policy out of its previous mire, and, if its implementation were to match its intentions, was promising. I witnessed the implementation failure during the first five years of this new policy. For example, the policy proposed that school–community "partnership compacts" would be developed and executed across relevant schools. These compacts were proposed to cover a wide range of topics – including commitments on staffing, curriculum and parental engagement – but ten years later not one such compact had materialised.

One problem with these policy documents is that they never grapple with the challenges of implementation. Even where the policies appear sound, implementation failure reduces them to yet another instalment in the Groundhog Day sequence. If an education "strategy" results in implementation failure, then it could not have been a true strategy. A proper strategy is not just good policy content and intent – it must grapple with what is needed to make it work.

Perhaps in acknowledgment of the lack of traction achieved by "Partners for Success" in its first five years, Anna Bligh as minister for education launched its second iteration in 2007, the even more hopeful-sounding "Bound for Success." Again, while the content was mostly unobjectionable, it was not compelling. It did not convince me then that it would achieve reform. Three years on, nothing has happened to change my assessment. It is just another episode in the Groundhog Day of Aboriginal educational reform.

Two Aboriginal populations

The late Maria Lane, an Aboriginal academic from South Australia, wrote an important paper in 2007 which she sent to me. Although I had never met her, I had the impression that she knew, from her own family background, the living conditions of people in severe disadvantage and that the main effort of her career had been to increase Indigenous participation in secondary and higher education, working in tertiary support services and researching – in relative obscurity – the changes in Indigenous participation in higher education.

The starting point of Lane's unpublished paper, "Two Indigenous Populations? Two Diverging Paradigms?", was four statistical findings from South Australia, covering the period from 1998 to 2006:

- The number of Indigenous youth in the Year 12 age-group rose by 60 per cent
- The number of Indigenous students actually enrolling in Year 12 tripled
- The number of Indigenous students gaining their South Australian Certificate of Education more than tripled
- The number of Indigenous students gaining good Tertiary Entrance Rank scores may have quadrupled.

Why was an increasingly large proportion of students succeeding in their education? To find the answer, Lane examined Indigenous social and educational history since World War II, paying particular attention to intra-state migration and

patterns of family formation. She concluded that the Indigenous population was splitting into two populations, which still
had kinship ties but were "each operating on completely different, in fact antithetical, dynamics, ethics and paradigms."
Not one to mince words, Lane characterised them as follows:

- A "Welfare-Embedded Population" which is risk- and
  work-averse, and benefits-, welfare- and security-
  oriented
- An "Open Society Population" which is opportunity-,
  effort- and outcome-oriented.

The origins of the Open Society Population, Lane argues,
are to be found in the 1940s and '50s, when Indigenous people
started leaving settlements for the city. The economic upturn
provided the first generation of Indigenous city-dwellers with
secure if menial work. Their children grew up with a work-
oriented ethos.

The second generation married non-Indigenous people to
a greater extent than their fellows in the settlements. The
level of intermarriage has since continued to rise. Children
with one Indigenous parent usually continue to self-identify
as Indigenous, so even if average family size might have
decreased slightly when people established themselves in the
city, the many mixed marriages greatly contributed to the
Indigenous population growth in South Australia.

The third Indigenous urban generation, which came to
tertiary age in the late 1990s and in this century, is participat-
ing in higher education at unprecedented levels. They enter

university directly after Year 12 on the basis of academic achievement, without the aid of Indigenous-specific policies or programs. The rise of this Open Society Population explains, according to Lane, the encouraging increase in successful Year-12 completions and university enrolments.

In the same half-century since World War II, many Indigenous people did not move, but stayed on settlements. The South Australian and Commonwealth governments abolished discriminatory legislation and extended welfare rights to all Indigenous people, and later instituted the CDEP "work for the dole" program, which provided further security for rural and remote communities. A Welfare-Embedded Population emerged, the members of which, Lane wrote, are:

> far more likely to see themselves as passive victims, and to externalise all problems either as the responsibilities of white bureaucrats, teachers, doctors or social workers (who "should do something about it") or as a product of their biology ("and there's nothing we can do about that"). Many, many "community" folk beliefs reiterate this belief in the immutability of the world and the externalisation of responsibility.

Of the Left-liberal ideology which informed government policy, Lane said that it:

> may have been intended to be collectivist, community-focused and independent, but degenerated into a protection for a work-shy, welfare-oriented population, an

44

ideology which has become an individualist parody of
its charter, parochial rather than communal, welfare-
dependent rather than self-determining.

Indigenous education policies in South Australia have,
Lane argued:

> been designed, almost exclusively, and with almost no
> positive outcomes, to cater to the needs of the Embedded
> Population. Much of this policy has reached exhaustion
> point, as has the entire paradigm of Dependence and
> Bureaucratic Control, on which the Embedded Popula-
> tion has centred its survival for nearly forty years.

Lane believed that the improved education outcomes of
the Open Society Population have occurred regardless of any
Indigenous-specific educational interventions (which Lane
scathingly characterised as being preoccupied with questions
of "relevance, cultural sensitivity, language, racist theories
such as learning-styles theory, appropriate curriculum, role of
elders or parents or community, self-esteem, cooperativeness,
need for outdoor activity, focus on sport, love of art, remoteness, etc.") and perhaps in spite of them.

As a result of the irrelevance of Indigenous-specific policies and the success of the Open Society Population, Lane
predicted that "there will be a shift away from a focus on
difference ... towards universal equal rights – which after
all, was the major goal of the 1967 Referendum, and which
is the cornerstone of Open Society Population ideology –

and from which Indigenous policy has been retreating ever since 1967."

Lane's analysis is hard to disagree with and her conclusions are hard to contend with. It is extraordinary and depressing that our nation has not come up with any better policies for Aboriginal educational advancement than the near-spontaneous process Lane has described. Surely assimilation is not the only road to success? What happens to discrete Aboriginal communities where people desire to maintain their language and culture? Is there no future for them except to assimilate or to languish in dysfunction and inexorable cultural pauperisation?

The ideal we have formulated in Cape York – that our young generations be able to "walk in two worlds and enjoy the best of both" – seems to be realised nowhere in our country's education of Aboriginal youth.

IF THE STUDENT HAS NOT LEARNED, THE TEACHER HAS NOT TAUGHT

The philosophy behind our approach is simple. We say, in effect, "Kid, it doesn't matter how miserably your environment has failed you. We will not fail you. We will take you where you are, and we'll teach you. And the extent to which we fail is our failure, not yours." We will not cop out by saying, "He can't learn." Rather we will say, "I failed to teach him. So I better take a good look at what I did and try to figure out a better way."

—SIEGFRIED ENGELMANN,
Teaching Needy Kids in Our Backward System (2007)

I have never forgotten my Grade 5 year at Hope Vale State Primary School. Responsibility for this former Lutheran mission school had been turned over to the state system before I started, but most of the teachers were still Lutherans during my primary-school years. There was no preschool and I started in Grade 1. My first year coincided with Don Schiewe's commencement as principal; he was a former school captain of what would later be my *alma mater*, St Peter's Lutheran College in Brisbane. You didn't have to scratch very far under the stern German exterior to find affection, high expectations and an abiding devotion to Aboriginal education. Schiewe would spend ten years at the school, a period when school attendance in Hope Vale was much higher than the Queensland average and the school was probably among the best in remote Australia – it certainly was in Queensland. It was Schiewe who set my ambitions for me: he remarked at the end-of-year school presentation night when I was in Grade 4 that he would "eat his hat" if this boy didn't go to university. Mr Schiewe could not know that he had at that instant planted a kind of belief inside me – one that my parents could not have planted, because they would scarcely have known what university was.

My father had received the standard Level 4 education provided to children at the mission, which armed them with a basic Bible-reading literacy (in Guugu Yimithirr as well as English) and a money-counting numeracy before they had to go out and work. Yet he was someone – as only one who knew him as intimately as I did could sense – who harboured a secret, unrequited love of learning. He would spend Saturday afternoons reading at his desk and tentatively writing in his notebook whatever remarks he would make at the next day's Sunday school or church service. He would have given a limb to have been more learned than his stockworking, crocodile-hunting, jack-of-all-trades and butcher-shop work and life history allowed. Most of his reading was religious tracts and books, and one day he built a small bookshelf which he fixed onto the wall, on which he placed his small hermeneutical collection (as in the Bible, not French post-modernism). There were scriptural studies, and books on

Lutheran history and theology, mostly old give-aways from the pastor or other mission staff. It was a bookshelf whose contents I would scan daily (and sometimes more often) in the vain hope that something new and interesting might suddenly appear there. But alas, I would have to settle for trying to find something of interest in a book that I had valiantly opened many times before. One volume I recall well was an instructional guide on the proper upbringing of children, manners and so on. It may have been from this that my father picked up Francis Bacon's famous saying, the first clause of which would become his salutary (and incessant) exhortation to me, my brothers and sister: "Reading makes a full man." From my earliest days I could be under no misapprehension about the value my father placed on books and reading.

My concept of a great teacher was shaped by Mr Schiewe and Neville Doecke, a fresh-out-of-Lutheran-teachers-college 21-year-old who would be my teacher in Grades 6 and 7. They were among the handful of educators with whom I enjoyed a close pastoral relationship, and who profoundly influenced my personal growth and intellectual development. Indeed, the relationship must be one of a kind of love. I suppose when any of us thinks of extraordinary teachers, it is a small handful who come to mind. My English teacher at St Peter's, Jane Greenwood, and history teacher, Mike Selleck, together with my primary-school teachers, compose my handful. The truth is that extraordinary teachers such as Mrs Greenwood and Mr Selleck would make the lists of hundreds of former students, such are their gifts; different students no doubt form special relationships with different teachers, but there are some teachers who touch the lives of legions.

A colleague who was a student of the broadcaster Alan Jones at King's College in Sydney once told me what an extraordinary thing it was to have Mr Jones teach him English. I well understood. A good teacher is a very good thing indeed. Brendan Nelson, when he was federal minister for education, launched a project aimed at getting people to recognise the great teachers they had in their lives. And one could appreciate his intent. However, this prevalent conception of the great teacher – which evokes memories of the handful of extraordinary teachers that one has had in one's own experience – tends to be misleading.

I first realised this when I reflected on my Grade 5 year at Hope Vale. My enduring memory is of a year spent in intensive English instruction. I think the school had struggled to find a teacher to teach Grade 5, so they hired an older lady who had once been a high-school English teacher. And we did English up hill and down dale for the entire year. At the time, it felt a little like doing football practice day in and day out. I particularly recall the program she used: boxed sets of cards which set out literacy exercises, published by the educational publisher Science Research Associates, which we called "SRA cards."

My schoolmates and I always stood a good chance of becoming literate. After all, the Lutheran missionaries had succeeded in instilling literacy from the early days of the mission in the late nineteenth century. To my knowledge, nobody from my grandfather's generation who had been brought up in the mission was illiterate. Everyone had attained a level of literacy sufficient to read the Bible, say. Most people were literate in English and Guugu Yimithirr. When I was a kid, the old and the young read comic books, cowboy stories and magazines. These reading materials would make their way around the village, read by all of the interested members of one household and then passed on to the next. *The Phantom* was, of course, premium.

But the literacy breakthrough that happened in Grade 3 and 4 was for me consolidated in that long, torrid Grade 5 year. When I went to St Peter's a few years later, my competitors in English were always but a few.

And yet I cannot remember my Grade 5 teacher's name. I have no recollection of her personality or her appearance. I can recall the names and have some memories of all my other teachers, from Grade 1 onwards, but not her. Yet I have always known that I received from this teacher tuition that was hugely beneficial. It is this that caused me to understand that the essence of the good teacher is above all the quality of their instruction – not their personality, their experience or even their academic aptitude.

In other words, the fact that there are exceptional teachers should not overshadow a true conception of what a good teacher is. A good teacher is first and foremost someone who provides effective instruction. As the recipient of a good education I have often overlooked the larger number of such teachers, tending instead to remember those teachers of exceptional talent or those with whom I enjoyed a special relationship.

In our reform work in Cape York we have put a lot of thought into the question of teacher quality. There is also a great deal of wider policy consensus around the necessity of producing high-quality teachers, particularly if educational disadvantage is to be confronted. The federal education minister, Julia Gillard, has made improving the standard of teaching one of her top reform priorities. As a result, the federal government is pushing a range of new initiatives aimed at transparent reporting of student and school performance, merit pay linking teacher pay to student outcomes, and establishing new pathways for teacher recruitment and registration.

But recruiting teachers to regional postings, and to remote areas in particular, will always be a challenge. These will always be hardship postings, so governments (and other school providers) will be stuck with a significant proportion of teachers being inexperienced, fresh-out-of-university graduates. These are also places where the average retention period for staff will always be low. If we can get teachers to stay for three years and more, we will be doing well. There are measures that can and should be taken to improve this, particularly in relation to the retention of school leaders, but our reform plans need to accept that three years for teachers is going to be about the average. We have to make it work within this reality: remote communities are not the Sunshine Coast!

The educational economist Andrew Leigh has produced important research on teacher quality in Australia and the marked decline in academic aptitude of contemporary teachers as compared to previous decades. Leigh's research confirms the now widespread view that quality of teaching is the

single most important determinant of academic performance. As a result, much reform discussion is focused on how
the best and brightest teachers can be recruited to the cause
of educating the most disadvantaged students.

I agree that teacher quality is the central issue when it
comes to educational reform. But the question of teacher
quality cannot be considered in isolation from that of instruction. Whether the teacher is equipped and able to deliver
effective instruction is crucial to the question of quality. This
is the formula upon which our reform thinking in Cape York
is premised: *Committed Teacher + Effective Instruction =
Quality Teaching*.

This is a subtly but crucially different interpretation from
one which focuses on academic aptitude. For those who see
instruction as but one among several qualities possessed by
teachers, academic aptitude will be critical. The view we have
adopted is that instruction is the key factor in determining
teacher quality.

On this view, teachers of average aptitude, if equipped to
deliver effective instruction, are capable of high-quality
teaching. Conversely, teachers of above-average aptitude
who are not equipped to deliver effective instruction are not
guaranteed to deliver high-quality teaching. (And on the
question of experience, we agree with Bill Gates that a teacher's capabilities will be well known within three years of
classroom experience, and that further experience will add
little to what is evident after this time unless the new experience involves systematic training in effective instructional
techniques.)

What then is the role of the dynamic teachers of the Knowledge Is Power variety, of whom Bill Gates was so admiring? Before we proceed, it's important to clarify the context of my discussion. I am talking about preschooling and primary schooling, what the Americans call elementary school. I think different considerations apply to middle and later secondary teaching. I am also talking about what is needed so that children are taught properly from the beginning, rather than being the recipients of remedial interventions later on.

Any new school-reform plan will, of course, need to take into account the fact that some existing students will be behind and will need help to catch up. It will also need to take account of the fact there will always be new children entering the year levels "through a side door" and who have not had the benefit of proper instruction from the beginning. They too will require remedial and catch-up measures. But the point is that our aim must be to institute proper instruction from the beginning of school life so that we're not constantly trying to make up for earlier failure.

By contrast, the Knowledge Is Power Program started with middle schools. They were dealing with students who had not received a proper early schooling and were behind. KIPP therefore had the challenge of engaging early teenagers in order to enable them to catch up.

The KIPP model is dependent upon highly motivated teachers, with higher than mean academic aptitudes, who make charismatic and dynamic teaching their goal. I don't think my Grade 5 teacher would fit that bill. And the problem for those of us grappling with education in remote Indigenous communities in Australia is that we will not be able to recruit this style of teacher in the requisite numbers.

We must have high commitment in any case. We will take what we can get in the charisma and dynamism stakes. But we will need to ensure that we can succeed even with teachers of average academic aptitude.

This is why I believe that a prescriptive instructional program in preschooling and primary schooling is needed. Teacher autonomy is not necessarily a good thing in itself (although educationalists and teachers' organisations tend to assume it is). The lower the expected aptitude, the more imperative is prescriptive instruction. Prescriptive instruction is not anathema to teaching as a profession; rather, it serves to give desperately needy students the kind of instruction they require at this stage of their education, and it will transform inexperienced teachers of average aptitude (including community teachers) into teachers who are highly skilled and knowledgeable about the full range of effective instructional techniques. Effective prescriptive instruction can also help out teachers of higher aptitude. Teachers do not have the time to do the logical analysis, curriculum design, field testing and modification of the presentation that is required to produce an effective instructional sequence.

My experience of the SRA cards that my Grade 5 teacher used must have played a role when, thirty-five years later, I became convinced of the effectiveness of explicit instruction, specifically the theories and methods of Direct Instruction, which have been published by Science Research Associates since the 1960s. Its chief architect is now a 77-year-old educationalist from the National Institute for Direct Instruction (NIFDI) and professor at the University of Oregon, Siegfried Engelmann. He has long been a professor, but it feels wrong to give him such a prosaic appellation. In my view Engelmann's contribution is the most profound of any educational theorist in the modern era and yet he labours in near-complete obscurity compared to Jean Piaget, John Dewey, Paulo Freire and Lev Vygotsky. Compared to these historical figures, Engelmann is as Darwin was to Lamarck. Except it is as if Darwin had written *The Origin of Species* and nobody noticed for thirty years. Those who know him call him Zig or Ziggy.

Ziggy

Engelmann became an educator and theorist inadvertently. While working in advertising in 1964 he undertook market research for a client who targeted young children and wanted to know how many exposures it took before children assimilated certain information. The dearth of research literature led Engelmann to set up his own tests using a focus group of children, including his own preschool twins and children belonging to his neighbours and co-workers. Thus was born a lifelong passion for education ("I didn't want to be in advertising. It didn't seem to be my shining star").

Engelmann was a relentless empiricist from the beginning. His research focused on the effects of intensive instruction on very young, disadvantaged children. The pedagogical formulae Engelmann hit upon in those early years formed the basis of his Direct Instruction ("big D.I." as his method is called), which spawned what is known as the direct instruction movement ("small d.i.").

It is not my aim here to provide a comprehensive account of Direct Instruction, nor of Engelmann's own story, which he set out in his 2007 book *Teaching Needy Kids in Our Backward System: 42 Years of Trying*. These are the main features of his teaching method:

- *Evidence-based*: It uses only scientific, evidence-based methods and materials
- *Efficiency*: Instruction is designed to teach more information in less time
- *Foundational skills*: It develops higher-order skills and complex reasoning skills in students by making sure that the prerequisite foundational skills of literacy and numeracy are in place
- *Homogeneous grouping*: Students are grouped and taught at their skill level
- *Sequencing*: Lessons are carefully articulated, with cognitive skills broken into small units, sequenced deliberately and taught explicitly
- *Accountability*: Programs are implemented with fidelity and students are regularly tested
- *Data-driven decisions*: Test results determine whether students are moved to a different group for instruction at their level
- *Pacing*: The material is neither too easy nor too difficult and teachers maintain student engagement by presenting information fluently

- *Clear directions*: Teachers limit directions to essential information
- *Correction*: Students are monitored daily and receive corrective feedback
- *Mastery*: Components of lessons are taught and re-taught until mastery is achieved
- *Remediation*: Remediation is implemented immediately when required
- *Positive reinforcement*: Student behaviour is managed with positive reinforcement
- *Professional development*: Teachers and aides are trained and receive ongoing coaching.

Engelmann joined Carl Bereiter at the University of Illinois and established a preschool with him, and the foundations of Direct Instruction were hammered out during this same period in the mid-'60s.

This was the time of the massive Head Start early-childhood program, established in 1965 as part of President Lyndon Johnson's Great Society "War on Poverty." Head Start is still around today, absorbing over US$6 billion per annum and employing more than 200,000 people and about three times as many volunteers. Its overall efficacy has long been in question, but the political difficulties of bringing the program to an end or of radically revising it are so profound that it has thus far resisted reform. (I would think that reforming Head Start is an even more formidable challenge than health-care reform in the United States.)

In 1968, the United States government commissioned

Project Follow Through, the largest and most expensive educational trial in history. It was designed to measure whether the gains made in Head Start could be carried over into elementary schooling. The trial eventually involved 180 schools and more than 200,000 disadvantaged students, and the initial evaluation period ran from 1968 to 1977. It was set up as a horse race between twenty-two educational models and sought to compare their effectiveness. The thinking was that successful models would be promoted across the country. Direct Instruction was selected for evaluation across twenty sites.

The 1977 evaluation, however, saw one of the greatest frauds ever in the history of so-called evidence-based policy, which bastardised the original aims of the long-run trial. A few other models showed modest improvement in some categories, but Direct Instruction placed first in all areas measured. Those based on Piagetian theories of "discovery learning" and Dewey-esque "learning by doing" had failed to produce improvements, not just in skills acquisition, but also in affective terms – that is, in terms of self-esteem and positive reinforcement. Direct Instruction succeeded on affective criteria simply because students who had succeeded in learning also gained in self-esteem, whereas those models that were predicated on these very criteria failed.

In short, Engelmann wuz robbed. The US Department of Education allowed the false conclusion to prevail that the outcomes of the Follow Through trial were inconclusive, and egregious bureaucratic and educational establishment machinations twisted the aims of the project (it was no longer a horse race when only one horse had won, rather than a group of horses coming over the line in close order, as the bureaucrats had wanted): it was retrospectively decreed that the intention had been to select success on the basis of individual sites ("projects") rather than models.

The chicanery was horrendous, and to read about it thirty years later, in another hemisphere, on the other side of the world, is still gut-wrenching. To most readers, that will seem an overheated reaction. But most people who read essays like this simply do not know what life is like down in the Marianas Trench of disadvantage. It is a world where strong ideological and cultural forces operate to reproduce perversity time and time again. It is not like the world at the sea-level of advantage where rational forces prevail. It is an upside-down world where black is white, and lies are truth. Of course Engelmann had invented Direct Instruction at the most inauspicious time in history for such an approach: the 1960s. Direct Instruction ran counter to almost every instinct of the ascendant educational thinking. Whereas Project Follow Through should have meant the demise of these progressive education theories – given the clear evidence of their failure – such an outcome was never going to be acceptable. They would continue to hold the commanding heights, as they do to this day.

By 1982, when he and Douglas Carnine published their *Theory of Instruction*, Engelmann and his lifelong colleagues had done what no one had done before in the history of education: they had hammered out a scientific theory of instruction. Whatever the objections raised against Direct

Instruction and the theory underpinning it, it remains to be scientifically refuted.

Project Follow Through and its aftermath was hugely depressing for Engelmann and his colleagues, but they regrouped and continue to this day to support schools across America with Direct Instruction and to serve disadvantaged children through their National Institute. Pugnacious and unyielding, Ziggy continues to work ten-hour days.

I wrote earlier that Direct Instruction had emerged at the most inauspicious time, but it should not have been so. Engelmann's Direct Instruction became available at the very same time that America's most disadvantaged people – African-Americans and Hispanics – gained their civil rights. The right to an effective education was surely at the core of these entitlements. Ziggy had offered to his fellow black and white Americans the opportunity to make good on Dr Martin Luther King's "promissory note" of entitlement to a full American citizenship. That it didn't happen on the scale it could and should have was a monumental travesty. Of the education establishment's culpability in this regard, Ziggy's bitter truth is this:

> It's framed as a moral issue but it's a masquerade. The moral issue that they advertise is like, "Oh, we care about kids, we're interested in their development, we're doing what's best for them, we're working with the community, we're doing all this peripheral stuff" and they're not doing anything that is functionally worth a damn. They just have to be called on that. And at some point some segment of

the whole educational establishment from measurement on down to training teachers has to recognise that it's a sham, and that it needs to be overhauled and centred around what it's supposed to be about. Not about how kids learn but about how we teach them. How we teach them most effectively and how we attend to their needs.

What it's supposed to be about: not about how kids learn but about how we teach them. So, then, how to teach?

Theory of instruction

In their 1999 book *How Babies Think,* Alison Gopnik, Andrew Meltzoff and Patricia Kuhl discuss their subject with reference to the recently emerged discipline of "cognitive science," which they tell us "has united psychology, philosophy, linguistics, computer science, and neuroscience, and given us a new view of the mind and the brain." The first idea they put forward is that babies learn like scientists. In fact, scientists are simply older children:

> The new research shows that babies and young children know and learn more about the world than we could ever have imagined. They think, draw conclusions, make predictions, look for explanations, and even do experiments. Children and scientists belong together because they are the best learners in the universe.

The second idea is the analogy of "the computational baby":

The Big Idea, the conceptual breakthrough of the last thirty years of psychology, is that the brain is a kind of computer. That's the basis of the new field of cognitive science. Of course, we don't know just what kind of computer the brain is. Certainly it's very different from any of the actual computers we have now.

The latter is close to trite, but I cite both of these ideas – particularly the idea that from the very beginning infants learn like scientists – because I interpret them to confirm what I think is the essence of Engelmann and Carnine's theory: *the minds of human learners perform logical operations,* apparently from the very beginning.

Learning involves the human mind taking in stimuli, identifying qualities of various stimuli and performing logical operations upon them on the basis of sameness, constructing rules and applying them to new examples of stimuli, and eventually forming generalisations that apply to examples that have never been experienced.

Cognitive scientists are astounded by the empirical findings of their discipline, which show how remarkable children are at learning from the very beginning. Child learning is so prodigious that these scientists are convinced it refutes John Locke's *tabula rasa* conception – the child as blank slate.

Instead the authors return to the *Meno* dialogue, in which Socrates discusses how humans can know an abstract concept such as virtue without having experienced it. His answer is that abstract concepts are not learnt from experience but are already known from a past life (perhaps an ancestor of the modern genetic-code idea, suggest the authors).

Socrates explains a recently discovered proof of Euclidean geometry to a slave boy pouring wine at a soirée. As he takes him through the steps of the process, the boy confirms them at each point and ultimately proves the theorem. "Socrates concludes that because the boy, who has had no experience of geometry, can do this, he must already know the proofs of geometry without being aware of them." Which leads the authors to the following conclusion:

> The new research shows that Socrates' stunningly coun-
> ter-intuitive idea was right: even tiny babies and unedu-
> cated children must know much more than we think.
> That's the first element in the modern answer to the
> problem of knowledge.

Nay. It doesn't confirm pre-knowledge. It confirms that human learners, even naive learners completely unacquainted with a particular area of knowledge, can perform highly complex logical operations, which can lead them to knowledge of matters beyond their experience.

The problem with cognitive scientists like the authors of *How Babies Think* is that they have no view on instruction – no concept of education – and therefore no sense of how an understanding of instruction illuminates child learning generally. Instruction involves both the empirical study of learners and their behaviour *and* the logical analysis of systems of communication and knowledge.

Engelmann and Carnine's analysis of cognitive learning breaks it down into three parts: first an analysis of behaviour, secondly an analysis of communication, and thirdly an analysis of knowledge systems. The analyses of communication and knowledge are purely logical, whereas the analysis of behaviour investigates the learner and how the learner responds to specific communications.

Start with the position that all possible sensory experiences – the universe of stimuli – that a child might experience can be logically processed.

Then the child, through her own scientist-like explorations of the environment as an infant, through the informal tutelage she receives from those around her, and eventually through formal instruction, starts to process all received stimuli within this logical system and to perform ever-more sophisticated operations.

Engelmann and Carnine identified the logical structure within which human learning is organised and grows. This discovery was not an empirical discovery, it was a logical discovery – though it is confirmed by empirical evidence.

Before turning to this logical structure, we should first identify what their theory says about how humans learn. Whereas cognitive scientists, and neuroscientists in particular, seek to identify the precise neurological mechanisms of human learning, Engelmann and Carnine start with a logical postulate. This means that when the neurological mechanism of learning is finally determined, it should possess certain specific attributes.

Engelmann and Carnine proposed a simple learning

mechanism with two attributes: first, *the capacity to learn any quality from examples*, and secondly, *the capacity to generalise to new examples on the basis of sameness of quality*. They explain:

> These attributes suggest the capacities that we would have to build into a computer that functions the way a human does. Note that we are not asserting these are the only attributes that a human possesses, merely that by assuming the two attributes we can account for nearly all observed cognitive behaviour.

The first attribute concerns *what* can be learned, not *how*. A quality is any irreducible feature. The assumption is that the learner can detect any quality, no matter how subtle, and is limited only by her sensory capacity.

The second attribute concerns *how* learning occurs. The learner has the capacity to "make up a rule" that indicates which qualities are common to a set of examples. This is the process of generalisation. Rule-making is assumed to begin as soon as examples are presented to the learner. In formulating the rule, the learner first "notes" the sameness of quality. Once the learning mechanism has "determined" what is the same about the examples of a particular concept, generalisation occurs.

There are two variables that account for what a learner learns: her environment and her own characteristics as a learner. Engelmann and Carnine's approach was to design faultless communications; that is, a means of communication that allows only one interpretation and which is capable of transmitting the relevant concept or skill to any learner. In this way the influence of the environment is held constant, leaving only one remaining variable: the learner's performance, that is, the number of trials it takes for the learner to achieve mastery.

The strategy of making instruction faultless (that is, unambiguous etc.) and then observing the performance of the learner is the basis of Engelmann and Carnine's theory. The following summary of the steps they take is worth setting out because it shows where logical analysis is used and where behavioural analysis is relevant.

First, they design communications that are faultless using a *logical analysis* of the stimuli, not a *behavioural analysis* of the learner.

Then, they predict that the learner will learn the concept conveyed by the faultless presentation. If the communication is logically flawless and if the learner has the capacity to respond to the logic of the presentation, the learner will learn the concept.

Next, they proceed to communicate with the learner and observe whether she actually learns the concept or whether she has trouble. This information (derived from a behavioural analysis) shows the extent to which the learner possesses the skills required to respond to the faultless presentation of the concept.

Finally, if necessary, they modify the presentation in response to the learner's behaviour. This modification is not based on a logical analysis of the communication, *but on a behavioural analysis of the learner.*

Five features must be embedded in effective communication for a learner to develop the capacity to generalise from examples:

1. Positive examples of the concept must be distinguished by one and only one quality.
2. An unambiguous signal must accompany each positive example, and a different signal must accompany each negative example.
3. Examples must demonstrate the range of variation to which the learner will be expected to generalise.
4. Negative examples must clearly show the boundaries of permissible positive variation.
5. Test examples, different from those presented to demonstrate the concept, assure that the generalisation has occurred.

The logic of this approach was not new under the sun. Yet Engelmann and Carnine failed to realise, during the nine years they spent developing *Theory of Instruction*, that it was a virtual facsimile of the methods set out by John Stuart Mill in his 1843 book *A System of Logic*. Mill called his equivalent principles the Method of Agreement, the Method of Difference, the Joint Method of Agreement and Difference, the Method of Residues and the Method of Concomitant Variations.

Mill didn't develop his system with education in mind and neither did he – or anyone else over the following century and a half – apply the system to education. At this year's

Annual Conference of the National Institute for Direct Instruction, Engelmann rued the long failure to realise that Mill had provided a basic structure for a properly scientific theory of instruction:

> He stood on the doorstep of being able to change the damn world by introducing logic in education so that people would have a sensible and theoretical basis for designing effective instruction for kids, [but] it never happened ... [The] basic assumption of all of this is: if learners are firm on the examples, if they can correctly respond to all the examples, they will learn the correct inference.

Implicit learning and explicit instruction

In his well-known 1997 book *Guns, Germs and Steel*, the American evolutionary biologist Jared Diamond wrote that "in mental ability, New Guineans are probably genetically superior to Westerners" and that "there is no hint at all of any intellectual *dis*advantage of New Guineans." Diamond's point was that the answer to the New Guinean politician Yali's question – "Why is it that you white people developed so much cargo and brought it to New Guinea, but we black people had little cargo of our own?" – had no basis in lower racial intelligence.

If basic learning is as Engelmann and Carnine's theory postulates, then clearly humans from all cultural and social backgrounds do a great deal of implicit learning. Formal instruction within one's own society and culture adds to this natural development, and adds to learning efficiency (to a greater or lesser degree). So the principles of instructional theory are inherent in much formal instruction, even if this instruction is not based on, or even aware of, these under-lying principles.

Let us differentiate between formal instruction and *explicit instruction* – that is, instruction devised with an under-standing of instructional theory. Explicit because the theory has revealed how learning works and knowledge grows, and the instruction uses this to obtain maximum efficiency in learning and (ultimately unlimited) learning growth.

Let us now differentiate between those Western children from the educated classes who have grown up in a society and culture where their implicit learning from their environment has made it highly probable they will acquire foundational skills in literacy and numeracy in the Western tradition, and those children who have not grown up in that environment and who have not had the same opportunity to implicitly learn the "hidden structure" (my words) of learning in this tradition.

This is one of the problems with those who resist explicit instruction: they condemn to ignorance children who have not had the same opportunities to learn implicitly. The American educational researchers Betty Heart and Todd Risley report a 32-million-word exposure gap between children of welfare-dependent families and children of professional families in their first three years (45 million words for children in pro-fessional families, 26 million for children in working-class families and 13 million in welfare-dependent families). There is a class blindness in the insistence of opponents of explicit instruction: Yes, if you're white and from a moderately advantaged background, then Whole Language may be fine. But if you're black and from the wrong side of the tracks, then it is not.

The Macquarie University professor Kevin Wheldall, developer of Making Up Lost Time in Literacy (MULTILIT), a "small d.i." remedial literacy program which we have used in Cape York Peninsula with marked success, once explained that in a normal cohort of students, the top quartile of students can be expected to learn to read no matter how they are taught, or how competently they are taught. The middle half will learn to read by whatever teaching method is employed, provided that they are competently taught. The bottom quartile of students will not learn to read without a phonics-based approach (in which letters are sounded out and connected up) that is competently taught. This bottom quartile will comprise children with innate or acquired learning difficulties and children from low-literacy backgrounds. Children from low socio-economic backgrounds and non-English-speaking backgrounds are likely to fall into this bottom quartile.

A phonics-based approach, which works for the bottom quartile, will also work for the remaining three-quarters of the students, provided that the more able students can proceed at their relevant learning levels.

The class and ethnic implications of this analysis are clear: Aboriginal children are, by virtue of their backgrounds, over-represented in the bottom quartile. The relative distribution of Cape York children compared to mainstream cohorts is very much skewed.

Typical schools teach to the middle and institute remedial programs for the (relatively few) stragglers. Where students are distributed according to Wheldall's model, this strategy produces more or less satisfactory results. The bottom quartile, however, need direct, phonics-based instruction, and the extent to which their schools make inadequate provision for their needs is the extent to which needless under-achievement occurs.

In Aboriginal communities, the approach to literacy must be qualitatively different because the majority of students are in the bottom quartile. It is not sufficient to modify the mainstream formula. Explicit, phonics-based reading instruction is imperative for Aboriginal students.

Four factors are often cited as reasons for educational failure or success: disadvantaged social and economic background, cultural difference, effectiveness of the instruction, and attributes of the students themselves. The fact of social and economic disadvantage is not within the school's capacity to influence – though if education reform is accompanied by a wider social reform, then those aspects of disadvantage that impede educational success can and should be ameliorated. Schools can take account of cultural differences, but again do not have complete control over this factor. Instruction is the one factor over which the school has complete control. Effective instruction can respond to student attributes to maximise achievement.

Explicit instruction is the ultimate "No Excuses" approach to education. It is based on teacher and school accountability for learning outcomes. Furthermore, it is based on the principle that there are scientifically established methods of effective instruction which, if used with fidelity, will produce learning success. Whether a student learns is not only a question of teacher commitment or effort, but also of whether the teacher has employed effective methods of teaching.

THE CULTURAL HEARTH

... a spiritual notion: the ancestral tie between the land, or "mother nature," and the man who was born therefrom, remains attached thereto, and must one day return thither to be united with his ancestors. This link is the basis of the ownership of the soil, or better, of sovereignty.

—JUDGE AMOUN, International Court of Justice,
Advisory Opinion on Western Sahara, 1975

Cultural and linguistic decline between generations hollows out a people – like having vital parts of one's viscera removed under local anaesthetic – leaving the people conscious that great riches are being lost and replaced with emptiness. In 2002 I wrote a letter to the then Queensland minister for education, Anna Bligh, setting out my thoughts on this subject:

> With each generation in Cape York there is a loss in cultural knowledge and languages. The loss is very marked between each generation. All communities in the Cape are heading down the familiar road of loss: knowledge is not being transmitted between generations and what is being transmitted is increasingly thin. The social prob-

lems consuming the communities compound this process of cultural pauperisation.

The problem that has emerged is that young Cape York people are ending up poor in Western education and knowledge and poor in their own culture and knowledge. They have not mastered their own languages and they are illiterate in English as well.

This rate of cultural loss is massive and is mostly occurring silently. Attempts at Aboriginal language maintenance have not worked, in my perception.

There is one thing that I am convinced of: that the long -term maintenance of Aboriginal languages and culture is completely dependent upon education. Without a high level of competence in literacy, it is not going to be possible to maintain Aboriginal languages in the long term.

There are three discontinuities in the Aboriginal cultural transmission and learning process that we have never properly confronted.

The change from oral transmission to multi-media transmission

In classical Aboriginal society cultural transmission and learning was orally based. Since colonisation much of this oral knowledge has been recorded by missionaries, colonists, government and anthropologists in the form of written documents, books, journals, photographs, film, tape recordings etc.

Oral transmission is no longer viable for cultural maintenance in the long term. It is not possible to teach and learn culture and languages through oral means. We have to face up to this discontinuity: our contemporary lifestyles and our immersion in a broader multicultural society with its diversions and pressures mean that oral transmission is simply insufficient to maintain our distinct cultures.

We have to move decisively to the use of multi-media methods of cultural recording and transmission.

The change from traditional lifestyle to our contemporary lifestyle

Classical cultural knowledge and its transmission was very intimately related to the land. Living on country and walking over the country, experiencing the country, was essential to the process of cultural-knowledge transmission. The intimate relationships with the land and environment that underpinned the traditional lifestyle are now past.

Our people's lifestyles have changed. We now live more sedentary lives in the communities, where people have jobs and kids need to attend schools etc. Also more of our people are mobile and spend more time in urban centres and working in other locations. The opportunities to live out on the country and to therefore transmit cultural knowledge have become increasingly limited.

Our contemporary lifestyle and living arrangements do not facilitate cultural knowledge transmission. The loss of intimacy with and experience of country is causing a loss of cultural transmission.

We have to confront the reality that our modern life-styles work against cultural transmission in the old style. And we have to confront the reality that our people will not return to the classical traditional lifestyle.

The change from our traditional knowledge and culture to the Western knowledge and culture

Of course our Aboriginal societies are now immersed in a broader Western (and, increasingly, global) culture and knowledge. Our traditional society, culture and knowledge are enclaves within a broader multicultural society – inescapably affected by this broader culture.

The external culture is, of course, powerful and the threat of loss of our own distinct identities and cultural diversity is an anxiety that is foremost in Aboriginal minds. The overwhelming force of the external culture, and its capacity to destroy our native cultures and identities, makes engagement in the wider culture a matter of great uncertainty and psychological trepidation.

My own view is that the way forward is to achieve a complete bi-cultural capacity. That is, for young Cape York people to be completely fluent in their own culture *and* the wider culture – and to move with facility and capacity between the two worlds. Even as we start to take the real actions that will preserve and maintain our distinct cultures for the long term (and there are no actions that are seriously doing this at the moment), we should see the external culture as our right and inheritance: it is a world heritage.

By getting our thinking (and therefore our policies) clear on a vision for a bi-cultural future, we can then embrace and engage with the wider Western knowledge and culture with greater confidence and certainty.

There has been a longstanding cultural hesitation about embracing and engaging with the wider Western and global inheritance (of knowledge) – and this hesitation has informed the quality and level of Aboriginal engagement in education in the past. This understandable cultural hesitation became an ideological resistance that has been counter-productive for our people, and this problem continued because we did not get our thinking straight and we did not confront the reality of our people now being irrevocably located within a multicultural world without walls.

This thinking gave rise to a project called Computer Culture, in the small community of Coen. The project trialled ways in which children, young adults and families could record and present cultural projects utilising various technologies. Families and community leaders developed a strong interest in their children's education through their involvement in cultural transmission. The Aboriginal principal of the Coen State School, Cheryl Cannon, described culture as "the hook" by which parents and families became active in the education of their children. It underwrote family and community support for subsequent welfare reforms relating to school attendance and readiness, the setting aside of money for children's educational needs, and the introduction and trial of the MULTILIT literacy intervention program.

It is important to understand that when talking about cultural education, I do not in any sense mean that Aboriginal education should be "culturally appropriate." From the beginning I recoiled from the notion of culturally appropriate education, and instead proposed "cultural engagement" as a better way of describing the intercultural zone where the global world and Western education meet the Aboriginal world and culture. In my 2002 letter to Anna Bligh, I developed these objections:

> We have gone through and are still in the throes of the "culturally appropriate" education era. But, if the intention was to ensure respect and recognition of Aboriginal culture and to make education sensitive and relevant, it became an alibi for anti-intellectualism, substandard educational programs and ultimately an excuse for poor achievement. Whenever the words "culturally appropriate" are invoked, it is invariably in defence of some poor standard – the words are never associated with something that is excellent and better than those things which are presumably culturally inappropriate.
>
> Many disastrous policies and programs have been tried under the banner of cultural appropriateness. Many of them are still around. It became an ideological catch-cry for the Aboriginal educational professionals, black and white, who used it to carve out an area of expertise and unaccountability for standards.
>
> My main problem with the concept centres on the word "appropriate," because this implies that someone is

to make a judgment about what is and what is not culturally proper. And this power to censor and prescribe was
ripe for abuse. It became a tool of anti-intellectualism –
people were being told what was "truly Aboriginal" and
appropriate and what was not. Arbitrary and political
rulings could be made which could curtail creativity and
ultimately limited the possibilities of what Aboriginal
education could mean.

The problem of culturally appropriate education was a
derivative of another more universal phenomenon: the educational fad that arose internationally under the banner of
"socially relevant education." Social relevance in education
sought to confine the content of curricula to the particular
circumstances of students, so that they could recognise and
identify with the world alluded to in their schooling. Therefore it frowned on a high-culture orientation for students of
the lower classes (the principal victims of this shoddy idea),
instead favouring keeping kids in the social and cultural
world of their origins. But it did not just eschew Shakespeare
in favour of popular culture; it also infected assumptions
about the educational aspirations of lower-class children. It
would be hard to imagine a more stunning instrument for
enforcing lower-class confinement than the notion of socially
relevant education.

Policy for a bi-cultural future
The education of a minority people obviously has great bear-
ing on the cultural development of that people. What children

learn during the most active hours of their most receptive years, the languages they speak and write, will shape their cultural identity and outlook. Children may receive informal cultural education in their family and community spheres, but it is hard to see how gradual cultural attenuation can be avoided if Aboriginal students' formal education in no way contributes to maintaining their culture.

At the same time, Aboriginal Australian students have a right to a mainstream education that does not handicap them on their life trajectory through the modern world. There is a tension – not a contradiction – here that needs to be resolved. To do this we need to understand the competing principles that give rise to the tension: high-quality education for Aboriginal students on the one hand, and the retention and revitalisation of Aboriginal culture on the other.

The first principle – high-quality education – is well understood in terms of the desired outcomes. But the second principle, and what it means for Australia to retain its Indigenous cultures, is not well understood.

The anthropologist Peter Sutton has pointed out that "Reconciliation" has gradually become more or less synonymous with reducing and ultimately removing the socioeconomic disadvantage of Indigenous Australians. The Commonwealth government's reconciliation policy framework has the name "Closing the Gap," and there are now legions of bureaucrats rebadging policy documents and programs with the new rubric.

That education is seen to be central to the reconciliation agenda is entirely justified. Aboriginal disadvantage in employment, housing and, ultimately, life expectancy can only be removed if education is fixed up. Patently it is the key to inclusion in the real economy.

However, the question of Aboriginal people's place within the Australian sovereign state has all but disappeared from the national agenda. There are many reasons for this. First, the social problems have become so deep and seemingly intractable that issues of culture and identity appear to be distractions. Not only distractions, but obstructive of social and economic improvement.

Secondly, the discourse on Aboriginal Australians' rights to culture and identity has been weak. Sovereign states are slow to recognise the aspirations for cultural survival of ethnic minorities. A political movement performing an analysis of the issues from first principles, to break through the wall of fear, indifference and misconception about Aboriginal self-determination, is needed. This has not yet happened in Australia.

Our vision in Cape York Peninsula is that our children be able to "orbit" between two worlds and have the best of both. It is the ultimate purpose of our reform agenda that our younger generations achieve their full potential, realise their talents and creativity, and have the confidence and capacity for hard work to enjoy the best of both worlds. To fulfil this vision, we work to restore social order so that families can grow in good neighbourhoods, parents and community leaders demand better education, and students are supported to reach and exceed national benchmarks and make the transition to secondary and tertiary study. Higher education is our goal.

The other part of our vision for individual mobility and engagement with the wider world involves the restoration of culturally and economically sustainable Indigenous homelands: places to which economically integrated future generations can return for longer or shorter periods of time. Cape York people have a working model for the return of land and economic development, but our thinking about long-term cultural maintenance is much less advanced. A thorough discussion of ethnic-minority policies is beyond the scope of this essay, but some issues need to be discussed to give context to education policies.

In a 2006 speech I proposed "Layered Identities" as a metaphor for diversity within societies. Having pointed out the inadequacy of the "melting pot," "patchwork quilt," "rainbow" and "salad bowl" metaphors, I said:

> There are two great problems with the dominant popular understanding of identity. Firstly, the identity of a group in society is assumed to be singular, arising from some salient characteristic such as ethnicity or religion. Secondly, the identity of an individual within such a group is also assumed to be singular – again arising from some salient feature of the group of which she is taken to be a member. This reductive approach to identity assumes that the individual or group has a single affiliation, or a principal affiliation that overrides all else.
>
> I have long considered that individuals and groups both possess "layers of identity." These layers include identification with cultural and linguistic groups; religions; places of

birth, upbringing, residency and death; local and regional geographic communities; regional, provincial and national polities; and professional, literary, recreational, philosophical and other sub-cultural groups. Each individual has many layers of identity.

I pointed out that the Nobel Laureate Amartya Sen used the term "affiliations" in his very similar concept of identity. I also noted that Sen had pinpointed the flaw in multiculturalism in Western countries:

Sen puts his finger on the main problem with multiculturalism, and this crucial insight flows from an analysis of what I have called layered identities and Sen has called "affiliations." "Culture," implying ethnicity and religion, is not the only layer of identity. There are many other layers with which individuals in a particular ethnic or religious group will affiliate. Societies that sponsor "cultural" diversity to the exclusion of other affiliations reinforce the problem of ethnicity or religion being seen as the single dominant affiliation. Cultures become identity blocs.

Sen's insight is that there is not a simple duality between two policies: "monoculturalism" and "multiculturalism." There is a third condition: "plural monoculturalism." Plural monoculturalism occurs where a policy of multiculturalism promotes culture as the dominant singular affiliation and ends up in a situation where there is a plurality of monocultures. This is the potential problem with multiculturalism.

Several thousand ethnic groups in the world have to find ways to co-exist within the approximately 200 existing sovereign states: this is a conundrum that leaves no room for separatism as a solution. In the case of this country, I remain convinced that Indigenous rights must be reconciled with a united, undifferentiated public citizenship of the Commonwealth of Australia.

In the long and ongoing debate about peoplehood, statehood and nationhood during the last two-and-a-half centuries, convincing arguments have been advanced in favour of the priority of those sovereign states that have emerged in the course of history. Ernest Renan famously rejected the notion that ethnographic criteria define a nation. Renan was descended from Brittany, which culturally and linguistically is distinct from the French majority culture. However, his definition of a nation was based on shared history and a willingness to share the future, rather than linguistic and cultural criteria.

Obviously Renan's thinki was shaped by France's traumatic loss of Alsace and part of Lorraine (which were ethnically German areas but loyal to the French state) to Germany. Renan's call for loyalty to the established states, published towards the end of the nineteenth century – the century of nationalism – was a sensible moderation of the romantic notion of nationhood, which, if taken to its extreme, gives rise to destructive fragmentation and irredentism.

Fragmentation and separatism is not a way forward for sovereign states. However, the metaphor of layered identities may give rise to the misconception that government policy is not obliged to support minority cultures within a sovereign state. If such an attitude informs public policy in Australia, Aboriginal cultures and languages will slowly (or rapidly in some cases) fade away.

I argue that government has a formal responsibility for the preservation of that cultural diversity native to the territory of a sovereign state. Today our nation does not have a realistic policy for Aboriginal culture. The development of such a program would require a discussion of some fundamental issues:

- What constitutes a people?
- What determines whether people remain distinct or are assimilated?
- How can government support the ethnic distinctness of the minority peoples of a country?

Peoplehood is, in the words of Professor John Lie, "a self-reflexive identity" that may be shared by thousands or millions of individuals. This self-reflexive identity is in principle entirely cultural and does not depend on common descent. An ethnic identity may be adopted by domestic or international migrants who move to an area dominated by another ethnic group; if the first generation does not completely assimilate to the local culture, the second generation of migrant families often does.

There are many sources of a sense of shared ethnicity: history, language, religion, economy and so on. Classical Aboriginal Australian thinking was very different to European thinking – so different that European concepts of "religion," "law," "economy" and so on are of limited use to describe Aboriginal culture – and classical Aboriginal concepts are very hard to translate into European languages. Similarly, concepts of ethnicity have varied not only from place to place, but have also changed through history. However, as contact between cultures has increased, a common understanding of ethnicity appears to be emerging. Today, a Yolngu person from Arnhem Land, a Welsh speaker from Britain and an Uigur from China would recognise each other's concerns for the political and cultural future of their peoples in a way that their ancestors would not have been able to.

In pre-industrial societies, small ethnic groups often remained culturally distinct even in the absence of political independence or national consciousness. The Estonian people, for example, were politically and culturally unrecognised for a millennium until they became independent for the first time in 1919, but lost none of their distinctness in all that time. Modernisation and industrialisation appear to have ushered in an era in which assimilation is much harder to resist. Today, culturally vulnerable ethnic groups face a stark dilemma: peoples that do not achieve independence or autonomy or some other kind of constitutional recognition, or at least develop a very strong ideological determination to secure their cultural survival, are likely to lose their distinctness and become assimilated.

The era in which culturally distinct populations do or do not make a claim to peoplehood appears to be nearing its end. Some peoples have achieved the favoured position of being the largest ethnic group of a sovereign state, which virtually guarantees cultural survival; other groups form a strong sense of peoplehood and achieve a relatively secure minority status, such as the non-sovereign Catalans of Spain. But many other ethnic groups are losing their distinctness. Minorities such as Aboriginal Australians have to make active choices very soon.

Minority peoples are naturally more vulnerable to assimilation, but small numbers are not an insurmountable obstacle to cultural survival. The Faeroese number approximately 50,000 and are constantly exposed to the languages and cultures of their European neighbours, and many Faeroese migrate to other countries (in fact, many members of this people have been and are "orbiting" throughout the globe as I hope Cape York youth will be able to in the future). But the Faeroese people resolutely resist assimilation and cultural extinction. To do this takes determination. It appears that populations that could potentially form recognised and viable peoples must quickly make up their minds about whether they are going to exist for more than one or two generations more. This is what I mean when I say that Aboriginal Australians must become a serious people.

The development and possible disappearance of a culture is the product of an enormous number of minute incremental changes in a large number of behaviours and beliefs of the individual members of that culture. I believe we should think of the Aboriginal Australian peoples as a population of individuals, who each have a particular relationship to culture and particular living circumstances. As a thought experiment, let us suppose that a very large survey or ambitious census was repeatedly performed in order to determine the current state and future prospects of Aboriginal cultures. Of each individual, an array of questions would be asked. Some of these questions would be specific to Aboriginal culture, traditional and modern: How extensive is a particular person's knowledge of languages? Of law? Of ancestral lands? And so on. Other important variables included in this checklist would not be culture-specific, but would capture the individual's social and economic capabilities: How much education and training has this individual received? Is she in employment? How good is her health? Has she managed to avoid substance abuse? Gambling? The importance of these non-culture-specific variables is that they significantly influence an individual's ability to retain culture, to pass on culture, and to develop and adapt culture.

This statistical exercise is a thought experiment, but one with an urgent present-day purpose: Aboriginal Australians need to be brutally honest about the threatening demise of Aboriginal culture. We need to face the evidence and be less rhetorical. The cultural survival of Aboriginal Australian peoples does not hinge on declaratory assertions that "We have always been …," that "We will always be …" The truth is that for Aboriginal peoples, the aggregate scores for the cultural indicators I suggested above are falling across the population, and it is this process that has to be turned around. And the general social and economic capabilities of our peoples have been falling or stagnant for decades, and are generally only improving among groups where culture is fading away. A crisis point is rapidly approaching.

To gauge our prospects, I suggest that we group the many factors that will determine our future into two categories: Cultural Determination and Socio-Economic Strength. Presently, Aboriginal groups like my people in Cape York Peninsula still have a lot of culture and determination to preserve that culture, but are socially and economically weak. Our culture is, however, vulnerable because cultural transmission is not working: as knowledgeable elders die, our culture becomes ever poorer.

It is hardly conceivable that Aboriginal people in remote areas will remain culturally rich but materially poor. Broadly speaking, there are three possible scenarios for the future. The future we were facing when we started formulating our Cape York reform agenda was cultural pauperisation combined with continued exclusion from the real economy and continued community dysfunction. This would be a miserable destination indeed for Aboriginal people. In the words of Maria Lane, "a substantial minority of Indigenous people have been going up the wrong track for forty years, and it is entirely uncertain if they will find their way back, to start all over again, but in a different world."

Successful economic and social policies in combination with undeveloped and unprincipled cultural policies may lead to a future of assimilation, where Aboriginal people are socially and economically on a par with the mainstream but no longer culturally distinct. This scenario is the best we can hope for with current policies and with current attitudes towards Aboriginal culture in Australia.

To achieve the optimal future scenario – socio-economic

equality and bi-culturalism – will require a significant change of attitude in Aboriginal people, Australian governments and the wider Australian public. The preservation of Australia's Aboriginal cultures is a goal in its own right – an indispensable element of reconciliation – but Aboriginal culture and languages are being weakened at an alarming rate. Yet this does not mean that Aboriginal people are indifferent to their heritage.

There is an apparent contradiction here. Why would cultural transmission be at risk if people value their culture? The answer, I believe, is that Aboriginal communities currently have a limited capacity to maintain their culture in an active way. To maintain a minority culture, people need capabilities, and – as Amartya Sen has shown – development of capabilities is a matter of equitable development, which requires the support of government policy. Cultural transmission requires a long-term government policy as well as strong determination on the part of Aboriginal individuals and communities.

The weakening of cultural transmission is the result of three factors that have been beyond Aboriginal people's control. First, the descent into passive welfare and substance abuse – and the ensuing chaos, which disrupts social and cultural efforts – is the result of policy mistakes made during recent decades.

Secondly, Aboriginal people's disadvantage has deprived them of the knowledge necessary to maintain a minority culture in a globalised world. Informal, oral handing down of knowledge to younger generations no longer works for vulnerable minorities.

Thirdly, Aboriginal people are at a psychological disadvantage when it comes to their culture and language. The choking of Aboriginal culture and languages did not end with the abolition of so-called protection in the 1960s: government support for Australia's native languages is still minimal. Government inaction and the Australian mainstream's disregard for Aboriginal languages act in concert to restrict Aboriginal people's freedom to express and maintain their culture.

It is entirely wrong to deny native minorities their right to remain distinct with reference to the (correct) principles of the inviolability of the sovereign state and undifferentiated citizenship. Regrettably, this is what some Australians do. The former Commonwealth minister Gary Johns and the anthropologist Ron Brunton asked the rhetorical question "A people any longer?" in a 1999 comment published by the Institute for Public Affairs:

> A major assumption of Aboriginal Reconciliation is that there is an Aboriginal "people." But does it really make much sense to talk about the "peoplehood" of Aborigines? … At the very least, reconciliation should mean an acceptance by Aborigines of the historical facts that have led to a single Australian nation, and the social and political consequences that flow from this.

This political and ideological resistance, accompanied as it is by mainstream indifference and Aboriginal disadvantage, makes it unreasonable to expect Aboriginal Australians to ensure cultural and language transmission is strong with-

out government support. The cynical suggestion that the maintenance of Aboriginal cultures and languages is the sole responsibility of the peoples themselves – in a fashion akin to the efforts of recent immigrant communities – must be rejected. There is increasing international recognition that it is a governmental responsibility to support – and be competent in – the country's native minority languages.

Because of the effects of historical and contemporary forces beyond their control, Aboriginal peoples need assistance to re-establish the social mechanisms of cultural and language transmission, and to establish modern, multi-literate modes of transmission. Government support for Aboriginal culture and languages would not be a concession to a minority interest, but a matter of equality; the English-language majority culture today receives more government support per capita than do Aboriginal cultures.

A big task lies ahead of all Australians to revitalise the transmission of Aboriginal culture. If we thought it necessary to convince the vast majority of Aboriginal peoples to become passionate cultural revivalists, we would certainly despair. But within each culture there is always a minority who take most of the responsibility for maintaining a culture. The majority of any ethnic group passively acquires some knowledge of their people's culture from the passionate minority, and most members of an ethnic minority learn the minority language if surrounded by speakers from an early age – not out of patriotic zeal.

A movement within the people to deliberately maintain culture and language is obviously necessary. But there have always been people deeply committed to Aboriginal tradition in our communities, and this has apparently not been sufficient. How are we to prevent the culture-carrying minority becoming untenably small in an ethnic group that has neither independence nor autonomy?

Government policy needs to recognise culture and especially language in a way that is not tokenistic. For example, Aboriginal languages need to be recognised as Australia's languages as far as is practicable. The unavoidable dominance of English is a pragmatic choice – not a fundamental judgment about the unsuitability of Aboriginal languages as media of communication, or about the undesirability of their widespread use. Low numbers of speakers, the absence of a literary tradition, the lack of a terminology to describe modern realities, declining transmission – none of these factors disqualify a language from being or becoming a language for a first-world modern society. Some of the languages of the Sami minority of Northern Europe are as small as Australian languages, and have a similar history of restricted use, but are nonetheless languages of instruction in public education. A member of the Swedish indigenous Sami minority said:

> The main reason I chose the Sami school for my children is that they should have a sense of belonging and be secure in their identity. I went to school in the '70s when Sami language was not allowed in school … I feel that I lost part of my identity when I didn't learn the language. I am happy that my children are given the opportunity to learn the language …

It is an indictment on Australian governments that there is probably not a single child of English-speaking Aboriginal parents who has been helped by government policies to reclaim his or her ancestral language. This is remarkable considering that Australia officially prides itself on its Aboriginal heritage and claims to be involved in a soul-searching reconciliation process.

Only through a combination of Aboriginal people's own resolve, social and economic progress, and principled government support for cultures native to Australia can our country's cultural national-minority issues be settled. What might this mean in practice? In disadvantaged Aboriginal populations, as much time as possible needs to be devoted to numeracy and English literacy in primary school. Over the next decade at least, students entering schools in depressed Aboriginal areas will, on average, have acquired fewer of the building blocks of English literacy and numeracy than mainstream students. Aboriginal students cannot plausibly close this achievement gap unless all high-quality time – mornings and early afternoons – is devoted to instruction that is tailored to their needs and abilities. The enormous socio-economic gap between the peoples of Australia – unparalleled in the world – necessitates a sustained and intensified effort to teach Aboriginal students Australia's majority language to mastery.

In our reforms for Cape York, we propose that the time from early morning to early afternoon be dedicated to explicit instruction in basic numeracy and English literacy. We propose that this domain be called "Class" and be clearly separate from another domain, "Culture," which aims to enable Cape York children to become literate in their own culture and languages, and to actively support cultural transmission between these children and older generations.

Together, the Class and Culture domains will make parallel English and local language development possible from early childhood. Superficially, our objectives resemble policies that have been implemented in regions where Aboriginal languages are very strong. What distinguishes our program is the uncompromising ambition that students become fully competent and literate in English and reach or exceed benchmark levels in primary-school subjects, as well as literacy in Aboriginal languages. We also plan to involve linguists and explicit-instruction experts in developing the written and digitised forms of our languages and the publication of more Aboriginal texts. This work will be urgent and difficult – the governmental neglect of our nation's languages has been worse than most people realise.

Finally, what is the place and purpose of Aboriginal languages and culture in modern Aboriginal communities? My answer is that they belong to our "cultural hearth." I noted earlier that global notions of ethnicity are becoming more similar, but the majority of peoples considered "indigenous" in the world differ in one important respect from "non-indigenous" peoples: relatively small indigenous groups have a strong connection to a clearly defined, relatively small area. This connection is of the kind that Judge Amoun refers to in the judgment I quoted from earlier: "a spiritual notion: the ancestral tie between the land, or 'mother nature,' and the man who was born therefrom, remains attached thereto, and must one day return thither to be united with his ancestors."

As long as Aboriginal peoples remain members of cultural communities that hold communal assets – traditional home- lands – the communal sphere will be an inescapable reality for individuals and their families. In my view the essence of the communal domain is identity and culture: tradition, history, language, law and education. This is what it will always mean to be a member of the "tribe." This essence is what the Maori leader Shane Jones once described to me as the "cultural hearth": the homeland of the soul.

THE DIALECTICS OF EDUCATION POLICY DEBATES

The children themselves eventually come to know that something is wrong, even if they are not able to articulate their knowledge. Of the generation of children who grew up with these pedagogical methods, it is striking how many of the more intelligent among them sense by their early twenties that something is missing from their lives. They don't know what it is, and they ask me what it could be. I quote them Francis Bacon: "It is a poore Centre of a Man's Actions, Himselfe". They ask me what I mean and I reply that they have no interests outside themselves, that their world is as small as the day they entered it, and that their horizons have not expanded in the least … For to develop an interest requires powers of concentration and an ability to tolerate a degree of boredom while the elements of a skill are learned for the sake of a worthwhile end. Few people are attracted naturally by the vagaries of English spelling or by the rules of simple arithmetic, yet they must be mastered if everyday life in an increasingly complex world is to be negotiated successfully. And it is the plain duty of adults, from the standpoint of their superior knowledge and experience of the world, to

impart to children what they need to know so that later
they may exercise genuine choice.
—THEODORE DALRYMPLE, *Life at the Bottom* (2001)

More than any other arena of public policy and academic discourse, the field of education is riven with debate. Education
is a key battleground between old ideological foes, nominally
from the Left and Right. There are many debates in education
that are intellectually substantive and which concern genuine
scientific and technical questions relating to teaching and
learning. But the muddy waters coursing through these rigorous debates are the currents of ideological struggle.

In my work in Cape York Peninsula over the past decade, I
have witnessed debates concerning "old basics" and "new
basics," "phonics" and "whole language," "child-centred" and
"content-centred," "literacy" and "critical literacy," "literacy"
and "multi-literacies." These discourses centre on fundamental disagreements about four issues: skills, creativity, critique
and self-esteem, and how these relate to knowledge and to
each other.

At the highest level of generalisation, the warriors from
the Right of the ideological field give priority to the acquisition of core academic skills as pre-requisite to the accumula-
tion of knowledge – and they range from carelessness to
suspicion on the matter of creativity, but harbour a strong
ideological aversion to critique.

Their opponents from the Left give priority to creativity
and critique. For the Left, knowledge is largely a motherhood
issue (although the postmodernist discourse about the

nature of knowledge contributes its own confusions) – but their aversion to focusing on skills has a strong ideological animus. At best they pay lip-service to skills acquisition, but they mostly see it as rote learning, which they believe kills creativity and stifles critical thinking.

On the matter of self-esteem, the two camps stand poles apart. The Left have developed a panoply of theories about and approaches to the matter of children's esteem, while the Right argue that effort and achievement are the source of true self-esteem.

This sketch paints the positions starkly when in fact there is often more nuance and complexity, and not every position falls neatly on either side of this divide. But my interest is in understanding the main driving currents under the choppy surface. The dynamics are often deceptive: a strong undertow can run contrary to surface appearances. I think the main currents in education concern the dialectical tensions between the core principles of skills, creativity, critique and self-esteem and their relationship to knowledge.

Before I discuss these issues further, I should briefly set out an extension of my views on dialectics and dualities, which I first outlined in my 2007 essay for *Griffith Review*, "White Guilt, Victimhood and the Quest for a Radical Centre."

The source of dualities

Dualities in philosophy, politics and economics are ubiquitous across societies and cultures: from the Yin–Yang of ancient Chinese tradition to the *dhuwa–yirritja* moieties of the Yolngu of East Arnhem Land, and the *wandaar–ngurraar* moieties of the Guugu Yimithirr of south-eastern Cape York Peninsula. Peter Sutton writes in *The Politics of Suffering* (2009):

> Aboriginal social and religious structures show a deep and ancient commitment to balanced oppositions, equal divisions. Two halves, four sections, eight subsections; male and female; inland and coastal people; hills and plains people; freshwater and saltwater people; light people and shade people; inside knowledge and outside knowledge; and so on. The list is vast.

What is the source of the dualities that we observe in the world? Whence comes dialectics – the interplay and transformation of such oppositions? Why are so many phenomena bifurcated, polarised?

What generates dualities is unclear. Three possibilities come to mind. The first is a spiritual, mystical or metaphysical source. The cultural manifestations of duality seem to have their origin in mysticism or spiritual belief. Hegel, for instance, assumes a metaphysical basis for the dialectical unfolding of history.

The second possible source is nature. This is what Friedrich Engels proposed in his incomplete 1883 treatise *Dialectics of Nature*. True it is that numerous natural phenomena exhibit a dynamic dialectical structure. Engels wrote his thesis well before perhaps the most fundamental example of dialectics in nature was identified: the wave–particle duality in quantum physics put forward by Niels Bohr, Werner Heisenberg and others in the 1920s and '30s.

Or might natural examples of dualities be merely the consequence of humans projecting a dialectics onto natural phenomena? The relevance of this question becomes clear when we identify the third possible source of dialectics: human perceptions and interpretations of reality. Dualities begin innocently enough. They begin because real phenomena are complex, and human understanding and perception of them necessarily depends on perspective. When we both look at the coin, I see tails and you see heads. Even where we fully appreciate the complexity and multi-sidedness of phenomena, human communication of this complexity is limited by my capacity to explain and your capacity to take in the explanation. Human articulation of phenomena is therefore – from the very beginning – highly susceptible to variations in perspective and standpoint.

At their innocent heart, different human perceptions of phenomena are usually each right in their own way. Neither of us is wrong when you see heads and I see tails and we each proffer (and prefer) our view of the reality of the coin.

Then upon this innocent core of cognitive and perspectival difference, interests come into play. Holders of particular perspectives cling to their view of the truth of what they perceive. They become attached to their interpretations. It then comes to be in their interest to insist on their point of view. Magnetic polarisation starts to increase as like-minded people form social and then political alliances against the views of people on the other side of the polarity. Social solidarity and alliances usually shake down to 51 per cent versus 49 per cent. The optimum group to be a member of is a 51 per cent group. It is not optimum to be part of a 90 per cent majority: there are too many people with whom to share the benefits of majoritarian power. The optimum state is to be a member of the barest majority: there are enough of you to constitute the *force majeure*, but you don't have to share the advantages of majority membership with more people than the absolute minimum. This is why elections in democracies come down to 51–49 per cent contests.

It is, of course, through debate and disagreement – discourse – that greater understanding of phenomena and their complexity is achieved. Knowledge requires dialectical intensity.

But there is a difference between that intensity which occasions the growth of knowledge and that which is driven by interests. The first kind of tension produces synthesis: growth in knowledge and illumination. The second kind is merely interest-based, zero-sum, ideological conflict. The two kinds are often inextricably entangled with each other. Perhaps only in the highest forms of rational debate – such as pure mathematics – is dialectical conflict interest-free.

Many debates about reality and its characterisation are relatively healthy and rational and we can readily agree that they should submit to scientific resolution. It is when interests are strong that irrationality and ideology come to hold an awesome sway, and science, even where it offers illumination, is gamely denied.

Skills, creativity, critique, self-esteem and knowledge

The debate between the advocates of whole language and of phonics in the "reading wars" was and is but a part of the broader conflict over the place of skills in education.

Rote learning in traditional education casts a long shadow over the question of skills acquisition. By the 1960s the ideas of John Dewey and the progressive educational movement were supposed to have gained the ascendancy and finally buried disciplinarian rote learning. B.F. Skinner's behaviourism was worse than passé; it was a form of barbarism that had no place in the future.

So when Siegfried Engelmann came along with Direct Instruction in the 1960s, it appeared to the proponents of progressive education to be an atavistic throwback to a primitive past. From the beginning the slur of traditional rote learning was thrown at Direct Instruction. Whatever data Engelmann had about how effective his methods were in teaching children was irrelevant. In answer to an interviewer's question in 1998 – "What were the negative things said about your method back then?" – Engelmann replied:

> All of the things that are said today. It teaches rote. It doesn't deal with higher-order thinking. It's contrary to the way children think. It is not consistent with development practices. It will be harmful to the children's behaviour in the long run. These kids will rebel later on, that they will regress later on and so forth.

I witnessed this knee-jerk response in the wake of my first visit to the Schoolwise centre operated by the Reverend Bill Crews in Strathfield, Sydney, where Professor Kevin Wheldall's small d.i. program, MULTILIT, is offered to low-progress readers from various public schools in the area. I had never seen teaching like the instruction these MULTILIT teachers were delivering at Schoolwise. It was dynamic, the teachers were extraordinarily skilful, the kids were eyes-on-the-teacher attentive, they hardly noticed our presence, no time was wasted, no child was left unattended for long, the teacher kept records of children's performance throughout the class, stopwatches counted words read correctly per minute from prescribed passages, the teacher dispensed positive reinforcement at every turn through their "a hundred smiles an hour" method. It left me breathless. You could have no doubt about the nutritious nature of the lessons these children were receiving; it was right there in front of you. And no child was missing out on the action.

"Rote," "boring," "inappropriate," "demeaning," "talking down to kids" and so on are not the descriptions that came to mind. And yet this is the standard feedback I hear about MULTILIT. Most people holding these views have not spent time in a MULTILIT classroom, and yet they can be absolutely categorical in their recitation of the standard denunciations.

Progressive educational currents set up skills as antithetical to creativity. It is true that creativity is something that comes from within the learner, and that, unlike skills acquisition, this is not just a process of learning from instruction. Creativity involves the nurturing, encouragement and draw-

ing out of the talents and passions of individual students –
but the acquisition of strong skills is not contrary to the
maintenance and growth of creativity. Indeed, the acquisition of many foundational skills through explicit instruction
and long practice is usually a prerequisite to the maturation
of creativity. The violinist must labour for years, doing the
hard yards and developing her skills, before she is in a position to demonstrate her creativity. Great creativity depends
upon mastery of skills, and the more exquisite the mastery
the greater the likelihood of genius in creativity. Pop guru
Malcolm Gladwell's "10,000-hour" rule in *Outliers* (2008) is
a salient insight into the importance of practice and the
mastery of core skills before true creativity and excellence
can be unleashed.

Robert Hughes's memories of traditional learning at the
hands of the Jesuits in *Culture of Complaint* (1992) left him
in no doubt about the nonsense of rote learning killing
creativity:

> It left no "time for smelling the roses", in that favoured
> phrase of American liberal educators (which usually
> translates as watching TV). This did us no harm at all. We
> either passed, or we failed and repeated the year, and the
> report cards went to our parents, whose feelings were not
> spared. We were made to learn things by heart and read
> them aloud, with the result that some of them stuck. (I
> have never agreed with the conventional belief that rote
> learning of texts destroys a pupil's "creativity"; actually,
> it enriches it by filling the wells of memory.) We bitched

about the discipline sometimes, but were on the whole
proud to be in the Jesuit cavalry and not the Christian
Brothers infantry.

Pace Hughes, one might point to a singular exhibit: the
most creative mind ever, Albert Einstein, whose memories of
schooling Manjit Kumar wrote about in his book *Quantum*
(2008):

> In 1888, aged nine, Einstein started at the Luitpold
> Gymnasium, and he later spoke bitterly of his days there.
> Whereas young Max Planck enjoyed and thrived under a
> strict, militaristic discipline focused on rote learning,
> Einstein did not. Despite resenting his teachers and their
> autocratic methods, he excelled academically ...

We can scarcely imagine life as a schoolboy in the Luit-
pold Gymnasium in the 1880s. (You think Zig Engelmann or
Don Schiewe were bad? Just think what their ancestors were
doing to poor Albert in 1888 – the year after they dispatched
one of their mob to the forsaken Cape Bedford Mission in
the Antipodes to put those poor Aboriginal bastards to the
stick!) But even in this case, the truth was that the dialectical
interplay of skills and creativity was key:

> Herman Minkowski, his maths professor at the Poly,
> recalled that Einstein had been a "lazy dog." It was not
> apathy but a failure to grasp, as Einstein later confessed,
> "that the approach to a more profound knowledge of

the basic principles of physics is tied up with the most intricate mathematical methods." It was something he learnt the hard way in the years of research that followed. He regretted not having tried harder to get "a sound mathematical education."

You sharpen your axe on the hardest stone. Practice makes perfect. No pain, no gain. No shortcuts, no excuses. And so on.

Plainly there is a staging issue for elementary education. Get the basic skills in first. Creativity will not be killed by giving priority to basic skills. Children have to develop their language skills, then they need to learn to read, then they can learn to write, and then they can learn numeracy. If they don't have these skills in place, they can't go any further. All diversions and impediments – every excuse, every suggestion that harm will come from such a focus, every appeal to "balanced" approaches to basic skills mastery – have to be removed. They are forestalling what is really needed.

The next source of resistance to skills is the notion that an early emphasis on skills acquisition stifles critique: instilling the basics is held to be authoritarian, subjecting children to rigid programming, constraining students' freedom and so their capacity to be critical and questioning. On this view, schools are seen as performing the function of formatting students to take their allocated place in the capitalist economy.

Again, like creativity, this is a staging issue. The acquisition of skills and knowledge should have clear priority over the fostering of critique, especially in the earliest years of education. Literacy is needed before "critical literacy." A widespread assumption – that if critique is not promoted in the earliest years of education, it will harm the prospects of students developing critical capacities in their later development – must be rejected. Full literacy gained through a formative focus on skills, and a solid grounding in knowledge, can and will foster the capacity for critique in higher education.

To begin to develop a student's critical capacity in early primary school is to impede the singular focus required for the mastery of foundational skills; such programs are diversions and must be steadfastly rejected by all those who want disadvantaged people to rise up in the world. Those who cling to these agendas don't consider whether their measures to arm children with critical capacities even succeed. Instead of critical thinkers and aspiring revolutionaries, these agendas (re)produce only lumpen, illiterate underclasses. It is hard to imagine any result more tragic – and more compliant with the status quo – than this.

The most dangerous capability is the capability to read. Literacy plus books are what spawn critique. More revolution was fomented in the Reading Room of the British Museum on the back of traditional rote learning in the course of a classical education in Germany than by any attempt to nurture juvenile critical capacities.

Students rigorously instructed in logic will be more formidable critics in their later development than ones who only possess opinions – and worse, feelings. Even individuals whose early personalities and temperaments tend towards challenge and inquiry will be ill served if they do not have a solid grounding in knowledge.

Even within the terms of leftist thinking, fostering critique in young people does not make sense. Genuine critique is the product of insights gained from knowledge and experience. The kind of critique that the middle-class Left are seeking to inculcate in the youngest of students is little more than teaching a certain form of manners. It is a certain ideological outlook that is inculcated in the form of (politically correct) etiquette. But surely true leftists are alive to the vacuity of this? It is mere bourgeois nonsense, having nothing to do with true critique. Those who peddle this kind of pedagogy are obscuring the fact that it is the experience of oppression and class constraint that is the origin of critique (and political action) – certainly not the teaching of criticism to the most impressionable of minds. As if these students, equipped with the desired manners, will be uniquely capable of rising above their actual class position to propose what the old leftists called "class suicide." Seen in the terms of the old Left, this kind of critical pedagogy is just the teaching of false consciousness, powered by moral vanity.

In education, no one is more responsible for this baleful legacy than the Brazilian educational theorist Paulo Freire. I have read *Pedagogy of the Oppressed* (1970) over the past twenty years, and even on a recent third reading it remains nonsensical to me. (You know how it is when you read something that is said to be seminal and you don't get it, but you suspend judgment, thinking its profundity must be beyond you, and so you give it another go later. After three goes, I'm afraid my initial impressions remain unrevised.) The educational equivalent of liberation theology – the bringing together of Jesus Christ and Karl Marx – Freire's writings are quite unlike the original critiques of liberal political economy produced by Marx and Engels, or even the critical theories of the Frankfurt School. His work has the kind of spontaneously inspired, proclamatory quality of Joseph Smith's founding of the Church of Jesus Christ of Latter-day Saints, and the mystical arbitrariness of Rudolf Steiner's Anthroposophy.

Yet few books have been the source of more diversion from the cause of education for the underclasses than Freire's. Schools of education in America and Australia have spent more time confusing future teachers with his texts (and worse, with the secondary extrusions of academics inspired by them) than they have in training teachers who can deliver effective instruction to the disadvantaged. Whatever Freire's achievements before the publication of his pedagogical views – and whatever his subjectively held concerns for the oppressed of the world – his contributions achieved the opposite of his intentions. He added to the perpetuation of oppression by diverting education away from what the oppressed really needed. By the time of his death in 1997, when he finally met Jesus and Marx in the afterlife (and they startlingly realised his cultivated physical resemblance to each of them), Freire had a lot to answer for.

The final field of dialectical conflict centres on the question of esteem. Almost all of the bad ideas advanced in progressive educational thinking since the 1960s are justified by an alleged concern for student self-esteem. The notion that education must be "relevant" to social and cultural circumstances was and is justified on the basis of, among other reasons, sensitivity to student self-esteem. The resistance to testing was and is justified on the basis of student self-esteem. The resistance to correcting students when they make mistakes is justified on the basis of student self-esteem. The refusal to hold schools accountable for proper reporting of academic progress to parent communities is justified on the basis of student self-esteem. Resisting the placement of students in ability groups for instructional purposes is justified on the basis of student self-esteem. Automatically allowing students to progress to higher learning levels without mastery of the antecedent level is justified on the basis of student self-esteem. And the list goes on.

That student esteem became the alibi for the agendas of educators is plain. It is not the students' self-esteem that is insulated by resisting data-driven teaching, including testing, it is the educators' accountability for poor outcomes, and what needs to be done about them. Andrea Boden, an educator visiting in Cape York this year, told me that students had no self-esteem problems if placed in mixed-aged ability-level groupings. She said, based on her experience in implementing Direct Instruction in the Gering school district in Nebraska, that the esteem issue is purely an adult projection. Students gain pride from mastering a lesson, but adults nevertheless assume shame will result if students are placed in ability-level groups. What is truly demoralising for students is to sit in lessons where their ignorance of what is going on, and their lack of mastery of the subject, is confirmed to them day in and day out. I think of the many Aboriginal students from Cape York who sit in secondary-school classrooms where the achievement gap is vast, not knowing what the hell is going on. Few thoughts are sadder for me than this image. This is the real esteem problem.

Which brings me to the identity pedagogy of the Indigenous educator Dr Chris Sarra. The director of the Stronger Smater Institute at the Queensland University of Technology, Dr Sarra is recognised as a leading figure in this field. There is much common ground between my views and Sarra's on Aboriginal education, but there are also fundamental divergences.

Sarra is a proponent of what I call a No Excuses approach to education, in that he strongly insists that the social, racial and economic backgrounds of Indigenous children should not be allowed to become excuses for low expectations and low attainment. There is no doubting Sarra's clarity on this or the correctness of his view.

Perhaps the difference between my concept of No Excuses and Sarra's is that I believe that just as educators have no excuses, nor should parents. To be clear: I do not disagree with Sarra's central insistence that educators must take the children as they arrive through the door and make successes of them, regardless of where they come from. However, simultaneous action is needed on welfare reform, including, at a basic level, requiring parents to take responsibility for school attendance.

The "strong and smart" philosophy of Indigenous student esteem and identity is the centrepiece of Sarra's approach to education. At first blush Sarra's approach appears attractive and sensible. The identification of indigeneity with low expectations and low achievement – and the wounds to esteem that these identifications may inflict – are a real and central issue in Indigenous education. This is a pervasive cultural problem for Indigenous people in Australian society.

However, although I strongly agree that the nexus between low expectations and Indigenous education must be broken, Sarra's approach is problematic. It is especially problematic in the public sphere. Educators invite many problems of identity politics when they make race the basis of pride and self-esteem. While the public promotion of Aboriginal racial pride might seem on its surface unexceptionable, indeed laudable, consider whether the public promotion of English or Anglo-Saxon, Greek, Arabic or Japanese racial pride would be well advised – even in an all-Anglo school, in the case of Anglo-Saxon pride.

While it is appropriate to celebrate diversity, I doubt whether the promotion of pride in specific racial identities is appropriate for our public life. I make the following points.

First, the Reverend Dr Martin Luther King's dream, when he confronted the problem of white racial supremacism in the United States, was "that my four little children will one day live in a nation where they will not be judged by the colour of their skin but by the content of their character." Just because the problem is perpetuated on the grounds of race does not mean the solution must be promulgated on the same basis. The fact that the problem of negative self-image has its basis in racial denigration does not mean that the solution lies in the promotion of its opposite: the explicit promotion of a positive racial identity. The positive solution lies in shifting individual estimation from race to character.

Secondly, the promotion of racial or ethnic pride is a tricky issue in a plural society: when does such consciously cultivated pride become chauvinism? In any event, the cultivation of such pride should be a matter of intra-group business – the business of the "cultural hearth," as I have described it – rather than something promoted in the public square. I challenge the assumption that institutions of the state – public schools – are appropriate places for the cultivation of racial esteem.

Thirdly, I recognise that the promotion of racial or ethnic pride may have immediately palpable effects on individual student and group consciousness, resilience and confidence. However, I query how long resilience and determination will last which has its source in the jingoistic promotion of racial self-esteem. There comes a point at which a more substantive basis is needed.

Fourthly, there is a danger that the promotion of pride in membership of a particular racial or ethnic group and its association with the positive qualities of being strong and smart (putting aside whatever equivocations one might have about these two qualities) ends up selling Indigenous students an illusion. Racial identity, no matter how confidently held, can't guarantee success. The surest basis for esteem in education is effort and achievement. It's not who you are or what claims you make; it's what you do and whether you have given your best effort.

The problems stemming from educators being commandeered into the task of remedying deficiencies in identity-based esteem become clear when one examines a centrepiece of Sarra's system-reform concept: his Accountabilities Matrix.

This matrix establishes how the education system should itera-
tively hold itself accountable for Aboriginal educational success
– from the minister down the line to the student. In 2004, the
Queensland government endorsed as policy a version of Sarra's
matrix adapted from his doctoral thesis. Teachers are required
to prompt their Indigenous students to reflect on self-esteem
as follows:

> Helping Indigenous children contemplate some hard
> questions:
>> To what extent do you truly believe you can be as
>> good as anyone in this classroom?
>> To what extent do you believe being Indigenous is
>> something to be proud of?

For a child grappling with identity ambivalence or imma-
turity – or indeed the very lack of confidence which is
assumed to be the problem – these questions are not just
hard, they may be uncalled for. The questions turn on the
degree of belief or pride ("extent"), and what is a child's
answer supposed to be? I am half-proud, or I am mostly
proud? Of course the politically correct answer, according to
the identity politics underpinning this question, is that one is
100 per cent proud! And one dare not show any ambivalence
or ambiguity.

But what if, like the artist Tracey Moffatt, one wants to be
acknowledged as a great artist who happens to be Indigenous, rather than a great Indigenous artist? What if one
wants to win a literary prize because of one's writing, not

because one has produced good writing for an Indigenous sub-category?

Interrogating children on the degree of their racial pride and strength is murky water. It might be appropriate as an intra-Indigenous exercise – for example, it may be acceptable for an Indigenous principal such as Chris Sarra to talk to Indigenous children about such matters – but great questions arise as to whether this is a legitimate subject for public education policy.

There are also problems with interrogating children on the extent to which they believe they are as good as anyone else in their classroom. Academic and other aptitudes vary in humans, whether they are Indigenous or non-Indigenous. Therefore it is misleading to make aptitude a correlate of membership of an identity-group. There will be perfectly confident and proud Indigenous students who are nevertheless average students. Challenging Indigenous students to compete with students from other backgrounds is proper – but how this is done without provoking simplistic identity politics and without selling illusions requires much more subtlety and careful, critical thought than Sarra's approach. Otherwise it just ends up being a jingoistic exhortation to racial pride. Role models are probably a surer way of supporting Indigenous children to deal with and challenge race-based problems of esteem than Sarra's attempt to create an identity-based pedagogy.

When as a ten-year-old I was shown by Don Schiewe a copy of Charles Perkins' autobiography, *A Bastard Like Me* (1975), the shocking title immediately galvanised a defiant pride in me that I have never forgotten. And when Senator Neville Bonner came to talk to our Grade 10 students at St Peter's in his three-piece suit and his shock of silver hair, I recall my pride. And when I watched Mark Ella and his brothers play Rugby better than the whiteys (oops, I mean non-Indigenous Rugby players), they provided the kind of morale a young Aboriginal man needs to navigate a private-school education. Self-esteem is important, but it is effort and achievement – indeed mastery – that is its truest source.

Schools as class-sorting machines

In a 1998 interview, Siegfried Engelmann explained that his antagonists in the educational establishment were voicing the same views in the late '90s as they had back in the 1960s: "They were saying the same things, exactly the same things. Nothing's really changed in education: it's fundamentally a sick system."

He went on to explain:

> They still use the same philosophy they used back when the school was supposed to be a sorting machine, when the ideal was to present Herculean-type challenges so they can weed out those that don't have the sand, the grit and the smarts necessary to be a professional. And the idea was to assume a kind of Darwinian notion that we have to select on the basis of genetic rigour or whatever, even within families those that ... can reach the 10 per cent. And fundamentally, although the rhetoric has changed a lot, the model has not, because back then the

idea was: you're presenting something to the kids, "Well that's too hard for most of them." Exactly! "They won't be able to do this." Right on! And so the idea came that they did what they wanted to do, but they just made it up as they went along ... And if the kids failed, tough luck!

On the interpretation taken in this essay, Engelmann and his colleagues had made a fundamental historic break-through when they discovered the instructional foundations of education: how it works, and how this illumination can be used most efficiently and effectively to accelerate learning and to succeed in teaching children who had hitherto been assumed incapable of learning. It was a democratising break-through because it moved child education from a "some will learn to the point of mastery and some will not" paradigm to a "we now know how we can teach all of them to mastery if we want to" paradigm. The Direct Instruction nostrum – "If the student has not learned, the teacher has not taught" – set a new standard and the highest possible expectation. The achievement of this expectation was not down to the learner, it was down to the educator.

Engelmann had developed an instructional method which could fulfil the expectation, provided that it was implemented with fidelity. His detractors had not, but they were the establishment, and in the absence of an alternative educational program that could democratise educational opportunity, they clung to their own ideological viewpoints – and if kids failed, tough luck! Thus they perpetuated the sorting-machine model of public education.

I discussed earlier in this essay the perversity that prevails in the Marianas Trench of disadvantage: what we see through the portholes of the bathyscaphe is an inverted image of reality. What appears progressive is actually regressive. What appears reactionary is progressive. The middle-class Left, peering out through the apertures and manipulating the robot arms of the subterranean vehicle, sees an upside-down world – and doesn't realise it.

This kind of perversity does not prevail in the rational climes of advantage: where the children of the middle-class Left are educated. The public schools to which they send their children are not like the schools down in the abyss. If I have learned anything about public education, it is that it is thoroughly class-sensitive in its provisioning. What it provides to middle-class kids at Edge Hill in Cairns is palpably different to what it provides at Cairns West, which is in turn palpably different to what it provides in Cape York. The quality is only as good as the strength of the interests of the class it serves. The public education system is still a sorting machine.

So why are the needed reforms resisted by the progressive side of the ideological divide? You have to wonder about this when an intellectual of social-democratic leaning, Andrew Leigh, makes the point in a 2006 essay for the *Griffith Review*:

Those who oppose the publication of test scores should remember who suffers most from an environment in which limited information is available about school performance ... Keeping test scores secret punishes low-income parents most, since they have fewer alternative sources of information about schools in the area.

He goes on to conclude:

Social democrats in Australia today face a similar rethink when it comes to education. The old producer-driven solutions have not worked. Our central focus must now be on better serving the consumers of education: young Australians. Getting the best out of our schools is the most promising way we know of to address our greatest social challenges: unemployment, poverty, inequality and Indigenous disadvantage. If we block innovation in Australian education, those who suffer will be children in the most disadvantaged schools.

My abiding interest in dialectics has led me to observe the strange near-convergence of conservative and Marxist analyses of this question: why progressives impede the prospects of the disadvantaged for whom they profess empathy and solidarity. As an English working-class boy done good, the pseudonymous psychiatrist and conservative author Theodore Dalrymple often comes close to a Marxist analysis of this progressive perversity (though he would doubtless be spluttering into his Earl Grey tea at the suggestion):

The educational absurdities foisted on the lower orders were not the idea of the lower orders themselves but of those who were in a position to avoid their baleful effects: that is to say, middle-class intellectuals. If I were inclined to paranoia (which fortunately I am not), I should say that the efforts of educationalists were part of a giant plot by the middle classes to keep power for themselves and to restrict competition, in the process creating sinecures for some of their less able and dynamic members – namely the educationalists. But if these middle classes have maintained their power, it is in an increasingly enfeebled and impoverished country.

I am more prone to old leftist paranoia than Dalrymple. I think the nub of the problem is captured in Paulo Freire's dedication in *Pedagogy of the Oppressed*, which reads:

> To the oppressed,
> and to those who suffer with them
> and fight at their side

The problem concerns those who are not oppressed but who, in Freire's view, "suffer with them" and "fight at their side." Who in the middle-class Left really suffers with the oppressed? And if the middle-class Left fights on the side of the oppressed, is it in the right fight? Do you really think, given the circumstances, that intervention rollback is the right fight? If your children were living in Yuendumu and you lived in Melbourne, and the only power you had over their fate was to say "yes" or "no" to the intervention measures, with all of their mixed political motives and mixed competence in design and implementation – and an honest broker from the field, like Bob Durnan, reported to you that the household your children were living in now had more food, and more money was being spent at the store – would you still think rollback was the right fight? Maybe roll forward, but not rollback surely. The point is that no progressive education academics would suffer their children to be given over to schools like those in Hope Vale or Aurukun. The solidarity is an illusion.

But there need not be consensus on the underlying explanation if the problem is so apparent: progressive thinking represents so much of the barrier to democratising educational advantage.

Before concluding this part of the essay, I should qualify what I have said about educators' resistance to true reform. I wish to distinguish between frontline educators and those responsible for generating and upholding reigning ideologies. According to my analysis of dialectical cleavage there is, firstly, an innocent and honest difference in perspective, and then interests come into play. Closer to the centre are the material interests of relevant participants, in this case the interests of frontline educators and their industrial representatives. While these interests are real, and they are the subject of much of what is defensively described as "teacher-bashing," I do not think this is the most significant barrier to reform. Frontline educators are highly sensitive to the needs of children, and if they can see how these needs can be better met, they will be attentive to them. The problem is the ideology-producers in the academies, and the ideology-upholders in educational bureaucracies. These people have investments in certain ideological tenets, which they vigorously champion. They are the source of the confusion and bad ideas that afflict frontline educational practice. If teachers resist reforms, it is because of this ideological production in the educational schools. In answer to a question as to what reaction he had expected from educators when he and his colleagues produced their instructional innovations in the 1960s, Siegfried Engelmann told an interviewer in 1998:

> I assumed that there would be some basis for them accepting it. I had no idea about the nature or structure of the psychology and educational community, although we had some rumbles all along the way. Every time we did something we were kinda surprised that when we would report it we would be so violently attacked. It became pretty apparent even by 1968, '67 that people were often far more interested in their personal investment and their personal status than they were in trying to find out what really worked with kids. There didn't seem to be honest pursuit on that level. There seemed rather to be a rhetorical level in which they hurled large slogans about; these were slogans that did not reduce into precise behaviour about what anybody should do and they were very opposed to things that ran contrary to their slogans or that they saw as a threat to their positions. And yet they had no data. I mean education I don't think has changed that much since the '60s.

And yet they had no data.

NO EXCUSES ON AN UNEVEN KEEL

The very idea of being in New York was dreamlike, for like many young Negroes of the time, I thought of it as the freest of American cities, and considered Harlem as the site and symbol of Afro-American progress and hope. Indeed, I was both young and bookish enough to think of Manhattan as my substitute for Paris, and of Harlem as a place of Left Bank excitement. So now that I was there in its glamorous scene, I meant to make the most of its opportunities.

—RALPH ELLISON,
An Extravagance of Laughter (1986)

In his interview with Eugene Robinson following his address to the NAACP, President Barack Obama revealed the flaw in his thinking about his relationship (and that of other successful and privileged African-Americans) with his own African-American community. Robinson's observation was that Obama had delivered his tough-love message "to a room full of NAACP convention delegates who are, by and large, highly educated and comfortably affluent – men and women who already have expectations for their children and know how to hold their elected officials accountable." His point: "Missing was the too-large segment of the black community that has been left behind."

Having confirmed that the diversity in the African-American community today was "all for the good," and that young blacks today were freer to pursue any of a full range of possibilities ("one of the ways that I think that the civil-rights movement ... weakened itself was by enforcing a single way of being black – being authentically black"), Obama then identified the one thing that African-Americans should not lose sight of:

> I do think it is important for the African-American community, in its diversity, to stay true to one core aspect of the African-American experience, which is we know what it's like to be on the outside. If we ever lose that, then I think we're in trouble. Then I think we've lost our way.

This is the crux of the white middle-class Left's class problem. It is the crux of the black middle-class Left's class problem: maintaining a solidarity with their lower-class brethren on the basis that "We know what it's like to be on the outside." It is this affinity that is the badge of credibility. It is their *bona fides*. It is the core of the middle-class blacks' fidelity to their identity.

My argument in this essay is that this solidarity is illusory and leads to false consciousness and moral vanity. This may seem a harsh analysis, but I persist with it not in order to be gratuitously insulting (after all, I am as susceptible to this delusion as anyone) but in order to expose its problematic core.

That the white middle-class Left has a sense of fellow feeling, sympathy, empathy – solidarity – with the lower classes is usually because Great-Grandfather came out of the bog or the coalmine in Britain and Ireland, and Grandfather was working-class to the bone. Grandfather laid the basis for Father to improve his lot and here we are now: middle-class professionals and academics and with our children attending university. This fellow feeling is not class solidarity, it is romanticism. It would be harmless if it just remained romanticism, but the problem is that it informs an entire cultural and political outlook – which in turn becomes highly problematic for the very lower classes who are supposed to be the object of this fellow feeling.

Come on, Mr President: you were never on the outside. You have worked with, have shed tears for and identify with people on the outside – but you have never been an outsider. Most of the younger members of your NAACP audience have also never been on the outside: this is Eugene Robinson's point. And if they once were, they are not now. The Harvard professor Henry Louis Gates Jr's arrest by the police sergeant James Crowley in his own home might have been a reminder that when it comes to racial profiling, a distinguished scholar and an undistinguished gangbanger share a solidarity of sorts, but life hasn't been all woodheap for Gates. The legal theorist Stanley Fish gave testimony to Gates' outsider status when he was a member of the Duke University faculty, but Shelby Steele's point about racial barriers being over-played applies here. Privileged blacks rarely experience the scalding pain of racism that lower-class blacks wear daily. Indeed, to the extent that a guy like Gates was an outsider in certain circumstances, he has without a doubt also been the beneficiary of insider status in very privileged circumstances. In more modest ways, so have I.

And we know from Barack Obama's biography that he was never an outsider in social or economic circumstance. He was only, at times, an outsider in *mentality*: and the key to his success was to have worked his way through his youthful crises of outlook and identity.

What is the problem here? Why do whites whose family histories have seen them rise up from the lower classes into privilege, and why do blacks who have made their way into the middle classes, get it wrong with their loyalties? Why does genuine fellow feeling end up being a problem for those at whom this feeling is directed?

There are a number of answers to these questions. I will eschew a leftist analysis at this time in favour of a straight liberal one, which I think sums up my thinking about what needs to happen if the underclasses are to be genuinely assisted to get out of poverty and take up a place of dignity. It is a view that was prompted by Kevin Rudd's back-to-first-principles discussion of Adam Smith's "self-regard" and "other-regard." Thinking about this, I hammered out in a recent speech my view on how the lower classes must needs rise up in the world:

> Self-interest is the most powerful engine for individual
> and social development, in other words, social progress,

in other words, social justice. It is when the most dis-advantaged in society have the opportunities to improve their lives in their own self-interest that change will take place. A whole lot of individual change animated by self-interest amounts to social change. Social change amounts to social justice. The provisioning of opportunity is indeed one of the key expressions of our common good; a product of social, altruistic and democratic action on the part of citizens and their government – but turning opportunity into capabilities and a better life is a product of enlightened self-interest. No anti-poverty or "social inclusion" aspiration will get anywhere without understanding that self-interest is the driving engine.

The problem is that the advantaged classes see the salvation of disadvantaged people lying in the advantaged classes' "other-regard" rather than in the disadvantaged people's own "self-regard." Altruism must be directed at igniting, and supporting with maximum opportunity, the self-interest of the disadvantaged. All other forms of altruism degenerate into welfare provision.

Maria Lane, as part of her analysis of "Two Aboriginal Populations," laid out a convincing typology of the class structure of Aboriginal Australia.

At the bottom is the *unclassed* or *declassed* group, corresponding with what Lane calls the Embedded Population ("perhaps a quarter to a half of the entire Indigenous population are still in this category. Ideologically, even more so. This is still the Indigenous population on which is focused the vast amount of policy attention, the population which is content to be dependent on welfare payments").

Then there is a *lower working class* ("a small, breakaway portion of the Embedded Population, which may be in irregular employment, and/or at any time involved in TAFE or even tertiary study, a population which is struggling to gain security and a more self-respecting way of life than is favoured by the Embedded Population").

Then a *working class* ("which is in regular employment, often inter-married, future- and goal-oriented, ambitious for their children, but basically wanting to be left alone by Indigenous policy-makers, forming the initial core of what I am calling the Open Society Population").

Then a *lower-middle class* ("semi-professionals and tradespeople, often young graduates, in secure employment and integrated into the Open Society, making sure that their children do well in school and go on to tertiary study – and keeping away from all policy-makers").

And finally a *middle and upper-middle class* ("usually professionals and established graduates, in permanent employment in government and academia, sending their children to private schools, thoroughly immersed in the Open Society but often seeing themselves as spokespersons and champions of, building their secure careers on the backs of, and gaining their kudos from, the Embedded Population").

Anyone with a knowledge of Aboriginal society will find it hard to refute Lane's analysis. And, of course, it is her description of the most privileged middle and upper-middle class that cuts to the quick of the Aboriginal Australian leadership malaise. This is the same problem that afflicts African-American leadership. I am as exposed as anyone to the scarifying truth of Lane's analysis. One can only be assured about whether one's leadership is not parasitic upon the misery of those in need by undertaking constant self-examination under a scorching light. Am I perpetuating victimhood? What am I doing to ameliorate people's present danger and suffering? Would I suffer my children unto the solutions that I propose for others? Why do I think that I need a job, to own my own home, to have sensible numbers of relatives visit me at any one time, for sensible periods of time, and so on – but that others might not? Do I have a proper justification for any double-standard or differential expectation? After all, I'm an Aboriginal, what's with the relativism?

Over the years I have often told people that there is a rough rule-of-thumb when it comes to examining the nostrums and prescriptions of the middle-class Left (black and white): whatever they say our people should do, we should look at approximately the opposite, because that will usually be the right thing to do. I once compiled a list of examples:

- They say substance abuse is a "health" issue and should be approached with tolerance; we say it is a behavioural and social-order issue and we need to rebuild intolerance
- They say education should be "culturally appropriate"; we say that this should not be an alibi for anti-intellectualism, romantic "indigenism" and a justification for sub-standard achievement and expectations

- They say we should respect "Aboriginal English" as a real language; we say we should speak the Queen's English and our own languages fluently and comprehensively
- They say our people need to be defended in a hostile criminal justice system; we say we need more policing to restore law and order in our communities
- They say our people are victims and must not be "blamed"; we say our people are victimised but we are not victims
- They say our people have rights; we say our people have responsibilities as well
- They say we have a right to passive welfare; we say we do not have a right to dependency and that we in fact have *a greater right* to a fair place in the real economy of our country
- They say that economic development and wealth creation is somehow antithetical to our identity; we say our culture cannot and will not survive as long as we live in the social dysfunction caused by economic dependency
- They say poverty is our main problem; we say passivity is our main problem because it prevents us taking advantage of opportunities to get out of poverty, such that the resources we do get are squandered.

And the list could go on. The point about this list is that it is based on the understanding that progress is not achieved on an even keel. You can see from the list that there is a prejudice here, a setting of the sails and a conscious weighting of the boat to one side. This is because we are not dealing with philosophical idealism: we are dealing with a real vessel in the real waters of political economy. And we're headed for hell. If our vessel must be turned, then we must work out where the sails are rigged wrongly and where the weighting needs to be switched. And yes, when the boat is turned, there will need to be constant tacking. Trying to maintain an even keel, waiting for the wind's direction to correspond completely with the direction we seek: this is not how it works.

Barack, you can't do No Excuses on an even keel.

I have no doubt that Obama strongly agrees with Geoffrey Canada's observations on progressivist thinking in public education, as reported by Paul Tough in *Whatever It Takes: Geoffrey Canada's Quest to Change Harlem and America* (2008). Discussing the debate between Richard Rothstein on the Left and Abigail and Stephan Thernstrom on the Right, Tough writes:

> [W]here did Canada stand? He agreed with Rothstein that the public-school system needed more money, not less. But on the other basic principles of the education debate, Canada found himself with the Thernstroms, on the Right. "I'm for vouchers, I'm for charter schools – I'm for anything that blows up the status quo," he told me. Canada felt that liberals' hearts were in the right place on poverty and education, but something – maybe it was their dependence on teachers' unions, maybe it was an overly idealistic view of how public education worked – had led them astray on this issue. "It is my fundamental belief that the folk who care about public education the

most, who really want to see it work, are destroying it."
Anyone who looked at the urban public-school system
not as an abstract idea but up close, every day, the way
Canada had for the past twenty years, would want to blow
it up, too.

What we need to consider is not just quality teachers but
quality teaching. In other words, effective instruction. President Obama should (and given his predilection for evidence-
based policy, so should Prime Minister Rudd) revisit Project
Follow Through, the world's largest educational experiment
aimed at trying to figure out what works, and satisfy himself
as to its meaning. It is not the case that educational methodologies trialled in the 1970s are irrelevant to determining
what works today. After all, it is not as if the problem to which
Project Follow Through was directed has been resolved in the
meantime. The same achievement gap is still there, and for
African-Americans it has worsened.

Perhaps the most gruesome argument for civic progress
in black America was put forward by the authors of *Freakonomics* (2005), the economist Steven Levitt and journalist
Stephen Dubner. They put forward an alternative explanation
for the decline in New York City's crime rates in the 1990s.
Rather than seeing this as a result of the broken-windows
policing measures undertaken during Rudy Giuliani's mayor-
alty, Levitt and Dubner declared it was due to the availability
of legal abortions following the United States Supreme
Court's decision in *Roe v Wade* in 1973:

So how did Roe v Wade help trigger, a generation later, the greatest crime drop in recorded history?

As far as crime is concerned, it turns out that not all children are born equal. Not even close. Decades of studies have shown that a child born into an adverse family environment is far more likely than other children to become a criminal. And the millions of women most likely to have an abortion in the wake of *Roe v Wade* – poor, unmarried and teenage mothers for whom illegal abortions had been too expensive or too hard to get – were often models of adversity. They were the very women whose children, if born, would have been much more likely than average to become criminals. But because of *Roe v Wade*, these children *weren't* being born. This powerful cause would have a drastic, distant effect: years later, just as these unborn children would have entered their criminal primes, the rate of crime began to plummet.

It wasn't gun control or a strong economy or new police strategies that finally blunted the American crime wave. It was, among other factors, the reality that the pool of potential criminals had dramatically shrunk.

Levitt's original 1999 academic paper, which gave *Freakonomics* the story that drove its explosion as a bestseller, was more explicit in its eugenics: it specifically referred to the fact that the poor, unmarried teenage mothers were (invariably) black. The theory would have remained gruesome if it was not subsequently shown that Levitt's economic analysis was flawed, which was in part admitted by Levitt and his original co-researcher. Adjusting for these errors, Levitt's critics repudiate the abortion–crime link while Levitt and his co-researcher claim that the linkage is reduced but still statistically significant. To the lay observer, a theory which would have been gruesome if it were true turns out to be obscene supposition.

Given that the authors of *Freakonomics* advance such bald propositions at will, I will risk putting forward one of my own, based on assumptions that I would argue are more compelling. The appalling crime and imprisonment rates of African-Americans could have been a fraction of what they are today if the young black children born in the forty-five years since the *Civil Rights Act* had been given the effective education to which their newly won citizenship entitled them; if the massive investment in Head Start had been followed by a comparable investment in what should have been the outcome of Project Follow Through. Even the children born out of wedlock to poor, teenage black mothers were children with the potential to learn and to make good in life. Siegfried Engelmann had a solution for them. Which story would we have preferred: a eugenics wish-fantasy or getting education right so that these children could have had a better life than their mothers?

EPILOGUE: STANNER REDUX

I am against both extremes, but I am much more against the pessimists than I am against the utopian visionaries. This at least can be said for them: they may simplify unduly: they may live and work for what turn out to be illusions; but as Mannheim, one of my teachers, pointed out, "illusions" begin as visions; they can be a powerful instrument of social struggle; a hard, working tool to re-shape the very situation in which the impulse to reform arises; and a brightly-lit goal for the will ...

The pessimists seem to me by far the more dangerous. They would probably prefer me to speak of them as "realists," and that I will do, although, being myself of a realistic turn of mind, I allow them no monopoly: I hold, with Herbert Read, that we are always free to try to make a new reality. They on their part seem to feel entitled to read with the utmost confidence from a history that has not yet happened. They purport to be able to stand "over" or "outside" history, and from some privileged knowledge, or natural insight, or inborn wisdom, or secret doctrine, to assure us (which I do not mind) and the Aborigines (which I do mind) that what

137

we are doing is a waste of time: they say that nothing will work because nothing ever has worked.

—W.E.H. STANNER,
"Aborigines in the Affluent Society" (1973)

Reading Bill Stanner again, one cannot but be struck by the way that matters canvassed by him in the 1950s and '60s – even in the 1930s – are essentially the same matters unresolved in Australia today. The depth of his insights, the sharpness of his perceptions and the quality and humanity of his discussion are lacking in our contemporary public discussion, which is cruder by comparison, and takes place as if the issues and the questions have only recently arisen. If only we could all remember how many "one-eyed hobby horses" governments have tried to muster in the name of practical improvement in the lot of Aboriginal Australians in the four decades since Stanner pointed out their contingent futility.

Blind to history, Prime Minister Kevin Rudd and his state and territory counterparts are once again marshalling herds of such horses (many of which should have been pensioned off in Slim Dusty's Long Yard) into columns under the banner of the Council of Australian Governments' "Closing the Gap" partnership agreement. Stanner will be shaking his head in his grave at such ahistorical folly. Of such policies, Stanner said, "they are all in part right and therefore dangerous. If all these particular measures, with perhaps fifty or a hundred other, were carried out everywhere, simultaneously, and on a sufficient scale, possibly there would be a general advance."

Stanner's hope was that Aboriginal people would be able to keep that which makes us who we are. Land rights was part of the necessary answer to this hope. It was not the wrong agenda. It was a necessary but by itself insufficient basis for the achievement of those hopes held in the past which failed to be fulfilled.

Stanner's questions were and still are right, although what he may have thought were their answers must be reconsidered.

I will chance my arm and say one thing about where Stanner's thinking requires crucial amendment. It concerns the place of the Enlightenment in Aboriginal ontology. The Enlightenment was not and is not at its core a European illumination: it is a human illumination. Its origins in Europe should not blind us to its human meaning and implications. The Enlightenment forced the Europeans to change their societies and cultures in fundamental ways. It forced societies and cultures beyond Europe to make the same change. The Enlightenment never mandated deracination or ethnic or religious assimilation or cleansing – all societies that have made this change have left space enough for religion and social and cultural diversity.

Darwin's Rottweiler, Richard Dawkins, is entitled to his argument that the Enlightenment and God are incompatible – but the world over, wherever the Enlightenment has shone its sometimes dim, sometimes bright light, social, cultural and religious mystery and idiosyncrasy remain and flourish. These societies split their personalities, allowing unto God, Voltaire and the abiding spirits of the Ancestors what are theirs.

Radical hope for the future of Aboriginal Australia, which honours the inchoate dreams of Stanner and Durmugam – if not in the way that they imagined it (nor perhaps in the way we imagine it) – will require the bringing together of the Enlightenment and Aboriginal culture. This reconciliation is not of necessity assimilation: just ask the Jews. The education of our children in both traditions, at the highest level of effort, ambition and excellence that we can muster, is, I have no doubt, fundamental to this hope. If our hopes are for our children, then we must take charge of their education.

RESPONSES

CHRISTINE NICHOLLS

Ludwig Wittgenstein wrote in his *Philosophical Investigations*, "A picture held us captive. And we could not get outside it, for it lay in language and language seemed to repeat it inexorably." In *Radical Hope*, Noel Pearson thinks, theorises and offers suggestions outside of the bleak picture of Australian Aboriginal education that currently holds sway. But ultimately it is in education that he places his hopes for the future: "I have hope. Our hope is dependent on education. Our hope is how serious we become about the education of our people."

As the principal of a relatively large Aboriginal school (fluctuating in the vicinity of 200-plus students) in the Tanami Desert, where I lived and worked for the best part of a decade, I too once shared the same hope. And while I still believe that education is of key importance, after many years of engagement in this area I have come to the realisation that the issues of housing, health and employment need to be equal, simultaneous and concurrent foci of government and private attention before education can bring about real and lasting change. These are by no means autonomous fields.

Until such a concerted approach is made, there will continue to be small, localised success stories in the area of education, but no broad, permanent change markedly for the better. Equally, there will always be those people whom French sociologist Pierre Bourdieu described as "*des miraculés*" or the "miraculous exceptions," those educationally highly successful children who emerge from the ranks of the working class, the underclass, the unemployed or from other materially insecure families, and who really "make it." Of this group, Noel Pearson is an example *par excellence* – perhaps the most miraculous of exceptions. And such exceptions are all the more miraculous because they serve to prove the rule. In order for large numbers, indeed a critical mass, of remote-area Aboriginal children to succeed in this fashion, housing, health and employment will need just as much urgent attention as education.

At Lajamanu School the Aboriginal and non-Aboriginal teachers mostly worked extremely hard, and the majority were highly competent. Together we were relatively successful in the education enterprise. In retrospect, however, I see that placing one's hopes in education alone is not enough. When children live in houses with thirty-plus people, they do not sleep soundly, there is nowhere to do homework, health and hygiene (physical and moral) become compromised, and if the children come to school at all in such circumstances, they are tired, listless and often hungry too. No matter how competent the teacher and no matter what whizz-bang teaching methodologies teachers might embrace, such children cannot be receptive learners. If they never or only rarely see their parents engaged in meaningful work, on whom do they model themselves? On what basis do they conceptualise their adult lives? These are simply realities.

Equally, if a significant percentage of the adults and children in any given community (even if it is a "dry community," as was the one in which I lived) suffer from kidney problems, heart disease as a result of rheumatic fever, eye problems such as trachoma, scabies, hepatitis, tuberculosis or even leprosy (which has been eradicated since the time I lived there), it is difficult for these children to put energy into learning and for their communities to give the necessary support to the educational enterprise.

Likewise, when 95 per cent of the children in the school have *otitis media*, leading to educationally significant hearing loss, then it is virtually impossible for those children to learn effectively, especially when instruction is in a foreign language. Year after year Lajamanu School was visited by teams of interstate experts who specialised in the diagnosis of hearing loss caused by *otitis media*. Up to ten people would arrive at the same time. These team members tested the hearing of every child in the school and the news, predictably, was always bad. This was, of course, a very costly exercise for the government, but *never* – not even once – was any funding put into actually fixing the problem. Eventually I wearied of this over-diagnosing, and, in desperation, wrote a submission to the Disadvantaged Schools Program and finally received modest funding to put microphones and loudspeakers into two classrooms.

Only a tiny minority of teachers in the school was trained to teach English as a Second Language (ESL). Over a period of more than a decade, only a handful of qualified ESL teachers was ever appointed to Lajamanu School, despite numerous requests. Nor, for the duration, were any qualified teachers of the deaf appointed to the school. There are no trained ESL teachers at Lajamanu School now. Inexplicably, the education department sees absolutely no need for teachers in these communities to have these vital skills as part of their educational repertoire. While English is now the mandated language of instruction for the first four hours of the day in Territory Aboriginal schools, these children are only just beginning to learn it. Children are expected to master initial literacy in a language that they do not understand – in other words, to learn a new language at the same time as acquiring literacy. Obviously, this is a "double jeopardy" situation, adding an unnecessary extra layer of complexity to their already compromised learning. Little wonder that school attendances have plummeted since the introduction of the "new" initiative.

Faced with all these major challenges, Aboriginal people also find themselves repeatedly confronted by illogical, inadequate and often ill-supervised government projects. Let me provide one example from the area of housing. In the late 1970s and into the early 1980s a builder was sent to live in Lajamanu, where he "worked" for four years, presumably on building houses for the local people. For this the man received generous government funding through the local Lajamanu Housing Association. In theory, he was also supposed to be training local men to continue building houses after he left. This did not happen.

Warlpiri people bestowed the nickname of "*Warlkanji-pardu*" upon this man. In English, this means something akin to Liar, Bullshit Artist, Big-Noter or Trickster (although the *-pardu* suffix has a slightly attenuating effect – "Dear Old Bullshitter" probably hits the mark). The man, big-talking but excessively lazy, had been employed by the Lajamanu Building Association to build accommodation for the citizenry of Lajamanu, most of whom were living in humpies or outdoors at that time. His grandiose verbal schemes for single-handedly revolutionising the housing situation at Lajamanu resulted in the construction of only half a mud-brick house, which in any case partially disintegrated while he was in the process of building it. Despite the waste of thousands of dollars of public money that had been allocated to ameliorate the parlous housing situation at Lajamanu, there were no repercussions whatsoever from the government or any other watchdog. Community members were clearly aghast, but their complaints were uniformly ignored or cast aside by authorities to whom they complained. Ironically, the man was fond of boasting to his mates that he had been "given a Warlpiri name," under the misapprehension that this Warlpiri moniker was evidence of his high standing in the eyes of the Warlpiri.

Government after government has raised expectations, dashed hopes and broken promises in situations akin to this one. Lest readers think that such episodes belong to the past, one need look no further than the current government's multi-million-dollar disaster, the Strategic Indigenous Housing and Infrastructure Program (SIHIP), in which the actual building of houses has been endlessly deferred. In stating this I am not blaming the present government alone, but drawing attention to the ongoing failure of successive governments in this area.

Earlier this year, Yirrkala School, in remote north-east Arnhem Land, was in the second round of stimulus funding to build a greatly desired language centre, but the Rudd government pulled the pin on the project, preferring, it seems, to allocate more buildings to city schools. In addition, despite Yirrkala being a nominated "growth town" and a site for education-hub development, it appears unlikely to benefit from the new National Partnership funding. In the two separate streams of funding that it has been allotted, it will receive $214,000 over 2010–11. Coincidentally, perhaps, DET is allocating this to cover salaries of cultural advisor positions. These were established in 2007 as part of the Remote Learning Partnership Agreement. So, basically, there is no extra money on which to base new programs aimed at "closing the gap." It seems that the first gap that needs to be closed is the gap between what governments say they will do, and what they actually do.

In this I am not singling out the current federal government, but making a general comment about all Australian governments. When it comes to Aboriginal affairs, each successive government, regardless of party affiliation, seems to glide into office with a Messiah complex. Each one seems to want to go down in history as the one who "fixed the Aboriginal problem." And in turn, each one fails, despite small, isolated pockets of success. This is not to say that all schemes and initiatives have been abject failures, but it is necessary to build on those small pockets of success. When governments repeatedly break agreements with Aboriginal people or refuse to take responsibility in terms of monitoring their own initiatives, this has a corrosive effect on communities and affects education, too.

If there were ever a case for bipartisan support on any issue affecting this nation, surely it is here, in the interrelated areas of Aboriginal education, health, housing and employment. While often politicians hold that their differences are major ideological ones, this is frequently not so. Rather, more often than not it is a matter of political grandstanding – if the previous government endorsed a particular project, method or approach, the current one won't, simply on principle. And so the depressing cycles of failure and disappointment repeat themselves, because effective measures are irrationally discontinued.

So while I agree that education is of utmost importance, it is hard to envisage long-term qualitative improvement in education without equal attention to health, housing and employment. Only then will it really become possible to implement a No Excuses framework – a highly desirable goal, but, unfortunately, probably not fully achievable at the present time.

Noel Pearson is spot-on when he writes that governments and their bureaucracies (and, by implication, others in the field of Aboriginal education) have no cultural memory. This applies, *par excellence*, to the field of Aboriginal education. While Pearson alludes to policy *failure*, educational successes are just as easily forgotten, and some policies are not given sufficient time nor enough governmental or systemic support to have any real chance of succeeding.

Bilingual education, for example, was constantly undermined by the Northern Territory education department in a range of ways, despite strong endorsement and support from Aboriginal communities and – albeit limited, for reasons that should be clear from this response – evidence of success. The greatest furphy about Aboriginal-language programs in schools is that they involve orality and literacy *exclusively* in Indigenous languages. In fact, in the majority of cases these programs were seriously subverted by the education department's failure to provide English as a Second Language (ESL) teachers to the Territory's Aboriginal schools. Virtually all of the Aboriginal schools in remote parts of the Territory are in fact bilingual – this is the daily on-the-ground reality – whether or not it is official policy. Therefore, whether or not official bilingual education programs are in place, children in these schools merit qualified teachers to teach them English. Since newly arrived migrant children receive such consideration, it is scandalous that Aboriginal children whose first language is not English do not.

In addition, a quality document is urgently needed for prospective ESL teachers working with Aboriginal students whose first language is not English, identifying the particular areas of difficulty the children encounter when learning English. To give just one example, at Lajamanu, where I worked, Warlpiri children had difficulty learning the correct use of both the definite and indefinite articles, because there are no articles in Warlpiri. Therefore ESL teachers need to teach directly to this area of difficulty. This is not to imply any kind of deficit; there are no articles in Japanese either, and sometimes even the most sophisticated and fluent Japanese speakers and writers of English experience continuing difficulty in mastering the use of English articles.

Furthermore, Aboriginal education in remote Australia is not entirely dysfunctional (an impression one might gain by reading Pearson's essay). Unfortunately, successive governments have forgotten the success stories just as much as they have airbrushed over their own policy failures. The latter becomes evident because these failures are recycled at regular intervals, in the guise of new schemes or initiatives. (I have observed at least three such cycles now.) There are curriculum and other education-related initiatives that have worked resoundingly well, and these need to be documented and published for use by prospective teachers in Aboriginal schools. Gathering and publishing stories of "best practice" in Aboriginal education is a matter of urgency, especially because of this endemic problem of faulty institutional memory syndrome.

I will provide one example from my own experience. After I had lived and worked at Lajamanu for at least five years, the Aboriginal and non-Aboriginal teachers in the school decided that everyone in the community would benefit from a clearly articulated school policy. To this end we organised a pupil-free day and invited every adult member of the community to contribute to the policy-formation process. A highly regarded senior educator working at the University of Western Sydney was asked to convene the process, to ensure, *inter alia,* neutrality. Many people turned up on the appointed day, including Aboriginal and non-Aboriginal community members, very old Warlpiri people, young Warlpiri people, the local Christian minister, missionaries, nurses and the plumber. The process of obtaining people's views was a fair one and people could speak in whatever language they wished – either Warlpiri or English. Interpreters were at hand for the monolinguals present. The entire day was recorded in order for there to be clarity about the issues on which consensus had been achieved. It took all day and many issues were thrashed out. The result was a policy document that gave me, as the school principal, a clear mandate to act in certain sensitive areas on which I had previously wished to act, but had met with resistance from certain powerful individuals in the community. Among these was the vitally important question of school attendance, which was strongly supported by everyone who attended the policy day. As a result, I could confidently begin work on improving school attendance, which at that point was sitting at about 65 per cent to 70 per cent.

After this, the local Aboriginal police aide, a senior man in the community, served, on my behalf, "Intention to Prosecute" notices to parents who repeatedly failed to send their children to school. Although the measure did not always proceed without a hitch, Lajamanu's school attendance soared to the highest in all Aboriginal schools in the Northern Territory, by 1989 hovering between 90 per cent and 97 per cent. This was more than comparable with that of non-Indigenous schools in the Territory. By that time, most absenteeism was explained by illness rather than truancy. As a result of this measure, one boy who continued to resist attending school with what seemed to be the constant excuse of "I'm feeling sick today" was consequently examined by the local health clinic. It was found that he had serious kidney disease. Thus this action probably saved his life.

The point about this story is that addressing the problem of habitual school truancy had (more or less) full community support, and could not have been achieved without it. The school also garnered community support because of the large number of Aboriginal trainee teachers working in it to deliver the bilingual program. Many Aboriginal people feel more comfortable in delivering their children into the hands of their own people, rather than non-Aboriginal teachers about whom they know little or nothing, unless they stay for lengthy periods.

This leads to one concern that I feel I must express about Pearson's essay: his lack of focus on the need for adult Aboriginal presence in schooling. I believe this to be essential for success in Aboriginal education, where the preconceptions of teachers often differ markedly from those they are teaching. Some of the current approaches to and orthodoxies about Aboriginal education run dangerously close to interfering with or even usurping the normal parenting process, and border on treating all Aboriginal parents and extended family members as if they are, *ipso facto*, dysfunctional. This is not so and if this (largely unspoken) policy direction continues, the effect will be disastrous.

The "lap-reading" program at Lajamanu School was one means of including Aboriginal adults in the school. Each morning, first thing, mothers would come along to the pre-school, transition and grades one and two classrooms, and read books to their children in either Warlpiri or English. It is essential that Aboriginal adults become part of their children's education, not just in some flaky "parents as partners" mode, which has turned into a meaningless mantra, but in ways that actually take older family members into classrooms to play a meaningful role. Such programs also allow families to learn what actually takes place inside those classrooms. It is not enough for Aboriginal children to have Aboriginal teachers, although it would also be a great advantage if more could be done to recruit young Aboriginal students into tertiary programs in the field of education.

The late Eric Willmot, an Aboriginal man and former director-general of education in South Australia, suggested that Aboriginal children frequently acquire what he described as "technical literacy" at school, but do not take on board the "culture of literacy." This is why many of these kids, even when they have been taught by methodology that includes phonics (as were the children at Lajamanu School), never actually become readers. In cultures where the intergenerational transmission of knowledge is predominantly by word of mouth, children need exposure to real books if they are to become readers. In the 1980s, with a few exceptions, there wasn't a single book in any Warlpiri home at Lajamanu. Incidentally but significantly, in the very successful lap-reading program, in many instances the mothers' own literacy levels soared, because they were reading to their children on a daily basis. Importantly, too, those mostly very young mothers were acting as role models for their children, just as Noel Pearson's own father had for his son by demonstrating his love of books, particularly the Bible.

Of course, phonics has an important place in the early literacy education of all young children, because they do need word-attack skills and they do need to know how to sound out words. I don't know of any teachers who would deny that, and I don't think that this area is as ideology-riven as Pearson would have us think. It seems to be more of an issue among politicians, academics and shock-jocks than it is among classroom teachers. But on its own phonics (and any other strategy for beginning readers) is not enough. No single approach to teaching literacy is enough, in isolation.

Encountering real books – that is, literature, not just commercial reading schemes that deliver scripted and frequently convoluted texts to provide opportunities for "pattern practice" – needs to be part of the equation. If children do not develop a love of books and literature, notwithstanding their mastery of the so-called "basic skills" of phonics and sounding out, they are destined to become functioning a-literates. That is, they will be able to function at a very basic level of deciphering individual words, filling in forms etc., but never develop that real love of reading that will lead them towards tertiary education and beyond. In this respect Pearson's basing his faith on one particular commercial reading scheme is simplistic and naive. Besides, the particular scheme that he endorses has real shortcomings, although that is beyond the scope of this response. Direct Instruction (or DISTAR) will certainly teach children to "bark at print," but that is not literacy in any fundamental sense. Direct Instruction, which has been marketed aggressively and effectively, has had limited success in inculcating word-attack skills, but more often than not that is because it's the first time ever that the child has been the recipient of one-on-one or small-group teacher instruction. I would reiterate that I am an advocate of phonics-based instruction for beginning readers, so long as it is one part of the teacher's arsenal, not the only strategy – because it can take a child only so far.

It seems that Pearson is unwittingly projecting a very narrow conceptualisation of what constitutes literacy in his essay. The great majority of successful teachers, including myself, utilise a range of strategies in teaching children how to read – designed to lead children into taking the next step, that of becoming literate, and "hooked on books."

There is absolutely no substitute for highly skilled, intelligent teachers. Attempts to "teacher-proof" (or even child-proof) reading instruction or any other form of instruction are nothing short of insulting to all involved and, for obvious reasons, are, in the longer term, bound to fail. Teachers need to make critically important educational decisions all the time. To resign oneself to supposedly teacher-proof alternatives smacks of desperation. Aboriginal children (and all children) deserve more than that.

Quality teaching cannot be disentangled from quality teachers as readily as Pearson suggests. This part of his essay is also somewhat contradictory. Earlier Pearson had acknowledged the critical significance of several inspirational teachers in his own early education. In addition, there was one teacher he does not remember very well, but nevertheless he describes her as being effective in a plodding way, despite being less than inspiring. He contends that this teacher was adequate, on the grounds that the learning materials she provided were sound. An alternative explanation is that the young Noel Pearson *survived* a year of being taught by this rather lazy-sounding teacher (we've all had one at some point) because he had already received the life-altering gift of exciting, motivating teachers who took a real rather than merely passing interest in his future. Moreover, it seems that this "average" teacher did not actively perpetrate any harm with respect to the children in her care – but it has to be remembered that poor teachers can have a seriously and permanently deleterious effect on impressionable young children, regardless of the particular armoury of instructional materials they use.

Substandard teachers are frequently the strongest advocates of the "culturally appropriate" curricula that Pearson so rightly scorns. Often the latter are simply an excuse for lazy teaching. Practically no teacher effort is required for teachers to set aside two and a half hours in the morning for children to write a two- or three-line "I went hunting for bush tucker on the weekend" story.

With respect to Noel Pearson's ideas about governments having a formal responsibility in terms of protection of Indigenous cultural diversity and languages, I can only concur strongly, and agree that both individuals *and* governments need to take a No Excuses approach to this, too. Indeed, Australia's remaining Aboriginal languages are in urgent need of legislative protection, otherwise soon there may be none left to protect.

However, I firmly believe that Pearson's idea of divvying up the school day into "Class" and "Culture" is not tenable. To allocate the less serious part of the day – by which time children in remote areas have become tired, bored and hot – to learning in and about their own languages and cultural heritage sends out a powerful negative message about their relative lack of importance both in the curriculum and in everyday life. Besides, language and culture are not "things" to be artificially separated or quarantined from learning generally. Nor can they be disentangled from the specific subject matter being taught, if one is committed to a serious approach.

There is a lot more that could be said in response to *Radical Hope*. Pearson deserves widespread, generous praise for rethinking the nature of contemporary Aboriginal education, and especially for aspiring to transform the lives of many disadvantaged Aboriginal children through education. Equally, his aspiration to hold on to Aboriginal knowledge and cultural practices, languages and traditions, some of which are experiencing severe strain, is of the utmost importance, as is his insistence that governments, as well as individuals, have critically important responsibilities in this respect.

Nonetheless, at times Pearson has a tendency to offer simple answers to some very complex questions. For example, it is well nigh impossible to isolate educational disadvantage from the closely connected areas of health, housing and employment; and there is no single commercial reading scheme that is capable of "doing the trick" when it comes to inculcating "cultural," as opposed to merely "technical," literacy. Nevertheless, Pearson should be commended for opening up the discussion in a way that is both urgent and necessary. If Aboriginal education cannot be conceptualised in a different way than it has been in the past, the cycle of failure will be repeated inexorably. Returning to Wittgenstein, it is vital that we do not remain captive to the cheerless picture that we have of Aboriginal education, eternally unable to get outside of it. While Pearson may not have sketched out an entirely new picture, he points to its very real possibility. I sincerely hope that Australians will rise to Noel Pearson's implicit challenge by responding to his provocative essay creatively, constructively and energetically.

CHRISTINE NICHOLLS is a senior lecturer in Australian studies at Flinders University. She is a former principal of Lajamanu School in Yuendumu.

CHRIS SARRA

Having just read Noel Pearson's *Quarterly Essay*, I regret that he hasn't had the time to take us up on our offer to visit at least one of our Stronger Smarter schools across the country. There is so much we could help him understand. I found his analysis of my work a little misguided and somewhat naive. While he tries, he clearly struggles to get the fundamental importance of how schools must develop and embrace a positive Aboriginal identity in a schools context, and surprisingly he offers virtually nothing on developing and embracing Aboriginal leadership in education. Perhaps this is symptomatic of a legal mind too much in dialogue with consultants, as compared to an educator in dialogue with a national network of educators.

Ultimately this doesn't matter when we consider his demands. Noel wants Aboriginal children to retain and sustain a sense of pride in their cultural identity. He wants them to be stronger. He demands a No Excuses policy that is determined to deliver academic excellence for our children. He wants them to be smarter.

There is always room in our ranks for others to join in our demand for a stronger, smarter future for Indigenous Australian children. He is welcome on my team any day.

CHRIS SARRA is the executive director of the Stronger Smarter Institute at the Queensland University of Technology. He was previously principal of the Cherbourg State School.

TONY ABBOTT

Even when he is on the other side of an argument, Noel Pearson rarely seems simplistic, partisan, self-congratulatory or ahistorical. He has lived the predicament of Aboriginal people struggling to reconcile their ways with modernity, thought about it with great sophistication, and written and spoken about it with unique power. Agree or disagree, it's hard to deny that he speaks with authority. That's why he's widely seen as a kind of modern-day prophet. Despite, for instance, concluding a thunderous 1998 oration with the call to be rid of "this putrid government," he had a much more complex view than the other, more predictably one-sided speakers on native title at that packed and roaring public meeting in Mosman. It was my first personal contact with Pearson. As the local MP, I found his attack on the then government was hardly endearing. It was pretty clear, though, even then, that Pearson understood how much more there was to Aboriginal disadvantage than simple racism.

When, a couple of years later, he began his long crusade against the unconditional welfare that was poisoning his people, members of that very government were among his most enthusiastic supporters. I was pleased, as employment minister, to have "whole of government" responsibility for commonwealth programs in Cape York because it gave me the chance to work with Pearson rather than just to agree with him. Pearson, I'm sure, already knew from bitter experience what I began to learn in that period between 2001 and 2003: namely, that it's much easier for well-intentioned governments to spend money than to make a difference. Still, over the course of several visits, including one camping trip with Pearson, Fred Chaney and some troubled Aboriginal youths from Aurukun, I came to think that perhaps the most serious obstacle to real reconciliation was modern Australians' failure to exceed the level of personal commitment to Aboriginal people that had been shown by the missionaries of former times. They had bled with them and bound their wounds. Many had left their bones in the communities they served. This generation's greater sensitivity towards Aboriginal culture has not yet translated into a more widespread inclination to spend long years performing thankless tasks in hardship posts.

In 2008, Pearson arranged for me to spend three weeks as a teacher's aide in Coen. In 2009, it was ten days assisting the truancy team in Aurukun. In his *Quarterly Essay*, Pearson commends the MULTILIT remedial reading program denounced as "rote learning" by much of the educational establishment. When I returned briefly to Coen, I found pupils who had been illiterate a year earlier writing simple short stories thanks to MULTILIT. In his essay, Pearson eviscerates the academic orthodoxy which makes "culture" an excuse for Aboriginal students' under-performance and even non-participation in education. At Aurukun, thanks to the truancy team funded and organised by Pearson's Cape York Partnerships through the welfare reform process begun under the Howard government, school attendance rates rose from about 30 per cent in 2008 to over 60 per cent in 2009. Of course that's still far too low. Undeniably, though, it's an important start.

Pearson's essay elegantly restates his now well-known positions on the importance of a standard academic education and on the need for Aboriginal people to be able to participate in the broader economy on their merits. That, though, is not his main point. Effective participation in wider society is more a by-product of the education that he wants for young Aborigines; it's not the main objective. Even in the most remote places, pre-prepared food, pay TV and four-wheel drives have had their inevitable impact. Aboriginal culture remains distinctive, but it is often but a distant echo of the high culture of traditional Aboriginal people. For understandable reasons Pearson is not very interested in preserving a contemporary Indigenous culture characterised by unemployment, substance abuse and domestic violence. He wants to restore fluency in traditional languages and the intimacy with country that can only come from traversing it on foot. In places where such a culture is no longer automatically passed on, Pearson thinks, education will be needed to create the mental aptitude and the critical mass for effective cultural transmission.

As is so often the case, just when he might have become pigeonholed, Pearson has the capacity to surprise both his backers and his critics. His call for a longer school day so that Aboriginal children can receive a sound general education is, of course, a challenge to the political Left. His bigger challenge, though, is reserved for the Right. Pearson wants the longer school day also to accommodate serious, sustained teaching in traditional Aboriginal culture: the language, lore and ritual of particular Aboriginal groups. Without an education in the "cultural hearth," as he calls it, Aboriginality may survive as an identity but it is unlikely to endure as a series of cultures. He's challenging Aborigines to become, in his words, a "serious people": like the Jews, perhaps the world's most successful minority, who have succeeded brilliantly in wider society while maintaining both their sense of identity and their distinctive beliefs and practices.

For all his consciousness of past injustice and of historical dispossession, Pearson is also an Australian. The civilisation that the British brought to this country from 1788 has ultimately benefited everyone, Aboriginal people included. Inevitably, Aboriginal people suffered grievously in the initial clash between modern and ancient cultures. Even so, British settlement brought immense changes for the better. As Pearson puts it, "the Enlightenment was not ... a European ... [but] a human illumination." This is the concession that Pearson makes to his non-Aboriginal fellow Australians. In return, the concession he seeks from them is a commitment to maintain Aboriginal cultures as living entities rather than as memories recorded in archives and artefacts stored in museums.

Although Pearson knows it won't be easy, I suspect he underestimates the magnitude of this task. The Jews are the most successful practitioners of cultural maintenance, but most Jewish people cling to the culture rather than to the religion; indeed, to liberal versions of it that might not pass Pearson's threshold test. Pearson concedes that individual

Aborigines might choose to assimilate, as many Jews have over the centuries. Still, real respect for Aboriginal people, he thinks, means empowering them to keep their culture as well as to change it or to lose it, if that's their choice. Government, of course, unlike Pearson, could not be partial about the choices Aboriginal people make.

The challenge, for those who have been Pearson's philosophical fellow travellers up till now, is to accept that biculturalism, at least for Aboriginal people, is a worthy object of Australian government policy and is worth paying for. That should not be too much to ask. After all, Western civilisation, especially its English-speaking form, has never demanded of people that they acknowledge a single immutable identity. Because it is unique to our country, support for Aboriginal culture is a responsibility of Australian government in a way that support for other minority cultures clearly is not.

In his final scripted speech as prime minister, John Howard acknowledged how far he'd come in his attitudes to Aboriginal issues. Undoubtedly, his late-flowering friendship with Pearson was a key factor in his personal journey from resistance to engagement. Over the years, Pearson has prompted quite a few conservative Australians to a change of heart. He's now inviting us to go a little bit further than the former prime minister was prepared to, but it's a project that we should be ready to support.

TONY ABBOTT was the shadow minister for Families, Community Services and Indigenous Affairs before becoming leader of the Opposition in December 2009. His most recent book is *Battlelines*.

PETER SHERGOLD

When I was the secretary of the Department of the Prime Minister and Cabinet, one of the more sensible things that I did was to engage Noel Pearson as a consultant. In truth, although the Cape York Institute for Policy and Leadership delivered a respectable report, the contractual relationship was not a great success. Pearson had too many things on the go and his formidably broad shoulders carried an increasing burden of responsibilities. No wonder that even then, beneath the hopefulness of his message, he was "prone to bouts of doubt and sadness."

For me, though, the appointment was important. Pearson was engaged as an adviser on social policy, not as an expert on Aboriginal affairs. It reflected my growing recognition that on the underlying themes of his challenging essay – the meaning of community, the complex balance of personal and state responsibility, the tragedy of learned helplessness and "social-order deficit" – Pearson had bold ideas which could significantly improve our understanding of welfare reform.

The consultancy was also a means to open a dialogue with the prime minister, John Howard, which helped to reframe the government's thinking. What Pearson offered was precisely what he attributes to Steven Wilson, the chief of the Ascend

Charter School in New York: he had come to a position which could and "should not be pigeonholed to the political Right or the Left."

When I persuaded Pearson that his voice might have greater political influence, I'd already spent fifteen years honing my own administrative ineptitudes in Indigenous affairs. I'd served in the Aboriginal and Torres Strait Islander Commission (ATSIC) for three and a half years and, later, as secretary of the departments of employment and then education. In those roles I had pushed for more effective programs to bridge the appalling chasm of disadvantage faced by so many Indigenous people. I'd exercised bureaucratic control with purpose and commitment. I'd genuinely believed that all Australians should receive a fair chance in life and that government policies could help to achieve that goal. It sounds, even as I write it, so touchingly naive. Perhaps my faith could be characterised as "romantic indigenism."

It is clear to the most casual reader that Pearson is not an enthusiast for Australia's public services, the "creators, filers and archivists of massive piles of history." It is not, as Pearson argues, that they retain no memory of policies; indeed, the remembrance by many individual public servants of the lack of substance behind so much vainglorious political rhetoric too often feeds hard-nosed cynicism. They smile, inwardly, at each "new" and "fresh" initiative. They know, because they have seen at first hand what most Australians do not, that self-determination has too often meant Indigenous communities organising their own second-rate services in Third-World conditions. The "legions of bureaucrats [now] rebadging policy documents and programs with the new rubric" know exactly what they are being asked to do.

Public servants are not bad people. Indeed, those who work in Indigenous affairs, both black and white, usually begin with a genuine desire to make a beneficial difference. That, I'm pretty sure, was my ambition. Only with time did I come to realise that goodwill too rarely translated into the benefits that I had anticipated. By the time I ended up in the Department of the Prime Minister and Cabinet, I was already painfully aware that in public policy the very best of intentions can result in the very worst of outcomes.

I had come to recognise that the making of policy (the sexy end of the job for most senior public servants) was nothing without its effective delivery. I was frustrated at how little the real-world experience of community-level bureaucrats influenced either the design of policy or its administration. I pushed hard for whole-of-government approaches centred on the citizen. I set up a Cabinet Implementation Unit to monitor whether government programs were being delivered on time, on budget and to expectations. I gave much greater recognition to the importance of project management. I had come, from my own experience, to the point at which Pearson now finds himself confronting Groundhog Day – that policy is vacuous unless it "grapples with the challenges of implementation."

It was from listening to Noel Pearson that I came to realise that something more profound was wrong. That failure goes to the heart of his essay on educational reform (which, I'm pleased to see, gives appropriate credit to the pioneering work of the Aboriginal academic Maria Lane). His message reverberates far beyond the schoolyard.

The problem is that no matter what the government policy, the means of delivering it too often externalises responsibility. Bureaucrats – along with social workers, case managers, lawyers, teachers and doctors – use their professional power to take control. They may not think so, but they do. The language might be that of self-determination, but the reality is welfare dependence.

Pearson taught me a simple but profound truth: if you treat people as dependents, they learn dependence. They become passive. That has been the essence of Cape York's welfare-reform advocacy for the last decade. It is the point at which self-awareness and moral responsibility meet. It is the axis at which the attempts to address social exclusion become the means to reinforce it.

Putting aside any debate about the details of Pearson's preferred educational model – such as the phonics-based MULTILIT literacy education program and the Computer Culture project – the essence of his approach lies in giving individuals and communities control. Rejecting the imposed notion of culturally appropriate and socially relevant education as ideological catch-cries for an approach which limits possibilities, Pearson instead looks to a bicultural future. His radical hope is that high-quality mainstream education can go hand-in-hand with the retention and revitalisation of Aboriginal culture.

I do not know whether demarcating "Class" and "Culture" in the Cape York classrooms will provide both the basis of economic opportunity and preserve the homeland of the soul. I can see both sides of the argument between Pearson and Dr Chris Sarra, but, in truth, I see their equally strong advocacy of No Excuses education as of greater significance than their differences. Others can debate these polemics. I have been only an "educrat" and an academic, and neither career, in my experience, offers much in the way of educational theory or the methodology of teaching.

What interests me most in Pearson's essay is the increasing intensity of his aversion to the progressives who "impede the prospects of the disadvantaged for whom they profess empathy and solidarity." Public servants – generally well-educated and well-motivated people – are part of that elite. Too often they, and many of the community advocacy organisations who work with governments, undermine the ability of individuals and communities to exert control over their own lives.

By the act of delivering government policies, program administrators often undermine self-reliance. Too rarely is self-interest, the ability to tailor government services to one's own needs, given licence – certainly not to those who are most disadvantaged and in greatest need of support. In Pearson's language, Indigenous Australians are victimised but they do not need to be victims. They are made so, in part by the way in which too many government programs and services are delivered as "sit-down" money.

Pearson's radical hope of educational reform will not be fulfilled unless the Aboriginal people of the Cape York Peninsula can take progressively greater control of their own lives. Whether they are seeking economic opportunity, living with a long-term health condition or struggling with a disability (or, indeed, all three), they need to be given greater opportunity to improve their lives by directing government support to their own needs. With that comes the requirement to recognise that their entitlements come with obligations, not least to live up to their responsibilities as parents. The local school communities require concomitant authority to continue to pursue their own approaches to educational philosophy, curriculum and governance. Individuals and communities need to be recognised as collaborators in the design and delivery of government policy.

These goals, to my mind, are not specific to Cape York. They apply not only to Aboriginal people and Torres Strait Islanders. They are not confined to the "education revolution." They are the essence of a more profound transformation in the way in which Australia seeks to create an inclusive and engaged society. Noel Pearson's message that the success of government policy will be determined by the mode of its implementation should become the catechism of public service. Perhaps that is too radical a hope?

PETER SHERGOLD was secretary of the Department of the Prime Minister and Cabinet from 2003 to 2008. He is a former head of the Aboriginal and Torres Strait Islander Commission and today heads the Centre for Social Impact at the University of New South Wales.

PETER SUTTON

There will likely be many technical disagreements over Noel Pearson's views on pedagogy. That subject is not mine, nor is it the focus here. Instead I will use this small space to try to understand the relationship between his critique of 1970s-style liberationist ideology and its remaining adherents, and the extraordinary levels of emotional heat being directed against Pearson and others who have mounted parallel criticisms in recent times.

Pearson's latest raid on Left-liberal orthodoxies will probably yield him a new crop of enemies, a fresh layer of angry educational people this time, to be added to those still reeling from his disembowelment of welfarist and segregationist models of social wellbeing for his people. As usual they can be expected to be among those who have found themselves no longer progressive and marginally placed critics of the established order, but old young people now embarrassedly holding more power than they ever dreamt of. Pearson's argument is that, as so often, some of the self-perceived liberalisations imposed by parts of this elite actually result in disenfranchisement of those most in need of compensatory assistance in life. After post-colonial embarrassment, we now have the potential for much post-post-colonial self-dismay.

In the context of an assault on "critical literacy," for example, Pearson analyses the "leftist" push for drumming up critique and creativity in young minds, while downgrading truly liberating skills such as the power to read. He describes it as the inculcation of a certain ideological outlook through the teaching of politically correct manners. It is the "the teaching of false consciousness, powered by moral vanity." Paulo Freire's once messianic afterglow as a '70s liberationist educationalogue is reclassified by Pearson as his "baleful legacy."

Such cattle-prod language was bound to get Pearson into trouble with those most deeply wedded to the positions and values he wants to carve up in his negative programs. Of course he also has massive positive programs, but they do not generate the flames of his heartily felt dumping on the Left-liberal orthodox. Similarly, his opposition to the use of race alone as a basis for self-esteem and pride, especially when so little actual achievement of anything may be required, must raise the hackles of those with a philosophical commitment to ethnic self-admiration, if not also those with even merely a venal interest in the commodification of Aboriginality as a tradeable essence. When people are told to be proud, but are not empowered to themselves create anything of which they can be proud, they must know, as everybody else does, that a charade is in play. That doesn't stop the show, of course. This is not surprising. The same transparent valorisations of outwardness also fail to curtail sales of *Who* magazine.

Pearson's essay covers much more than these topics, of course.

I'll propose some reasons why I think the temperature around these issues has gone up so far so fast, and why so much of the debate is now being conducted in *ad hominem* and *ad feminam* terms. It's true that some angry people have used some strong language. Pearson, Marcia Langton and myself are not alone there. If you stick your head up, someone will want to kick it, as Doug Anthony would say. You say *moral vanity*, and I'll hit back with *moral panic*. This much can be very schoolyard. But there is a lot more to it.

This is because the post-orthodox critique threatens more than mere opinions, entrenched or otherwise. It threatens moral selves. It is a danger not just to freedom from self-doubt, but to many people's ethical self-regard, to their biographies, to their legacies. So many now in this position of fight or flight were once idealistic young people who gave much of their lives, especially after the early 1970s, to the high hopes of the principles and processes that are now, even if only selectively, under such a cloud. This applies to people in Aboriginal affairs, but it also applies to many other departments of Australian life. This much of their potential for resistance may seem purely secular, purely psychological, but for many it goes further. It is often deep-seated faith. The failure of such an idealism can be a small death of the spirit.

Like other devotional fortresses, this one doesn't rest much on empirical evidence. This is why empirical evidence is such a weak threat to its comforts.

This idealism is the sort of faith that allows one to be a transcendental utopian at the same time as being a materialist atheist. The first driving force in its physiology is negative rather than positive; the central spring is criticism. One's goodness is first demonstrated by the badness of others, and by one's manifest skills in exposing it. It is not, primarily, a matter of one's character. Character is out of style, although not with Pearson.

The cliché of "perpetual protest mode" is snug here. Protest is at times a perpetual-motion machine, feeding itself but never satisfied, a dog happily chasing its tail in anger. The film *Five Easy Pieces* (1970) comes to mind. Terry and Palm are hitchhikers in the back seat, having been picked up by Bobby (Jack Nicholson) and Rayette (Karen Black):

TERRY: In my personal observation, I think that more people are neat than are clean …

PALM: In my personal thing, I don't see that. I'm seeing more filth. A lot of filth. What they need to do every day, no, once in a while, is a cockroach thing, where they spray the homes. And uh … can you imagine, if their doors were painted a pretty color, and they had a pot outside, with …

TERRY: Yeah, it could be adorable …

PALM: And they picked up! I mean, it wouldn't be filthy, with Coke bottles and whiskey, and those signs everywhere …

She gestures angrily out the window at the roadside billboards.

PALM (CONT'D): ... they oughta be erased! All those signs, selling crap, and more crap, and, I don't know, it's disgusting, I don't even want to talk about it!

BOBBY: Well ...

PALM: It's just filthy. People are dirty. I think that's the biggest thing that's wrong with people. I think they wouldn't be as violent if they were clean, because then they wouldn't have anybody to pick on ... Oofh ... Dirt ...

RAYETTE: Well ...

PALM: Not dirt. See, dirt isn't bad. It's filth. Filth is bad. That's what starts maggots and riots ...

Utopian and negativist at the same time, the '70s dreamer and freedom-fighter often preferred to be agin the government, not part of it. But middle-aged Boomery and the inexorability of the mortgage have brought a rise up the political and bureaucratic and academic food chains, the chance to do things, and thus the overweening threat of facing reality. Success has created an unprecedented opportunity for the experience of failure. No wonder collars are hot.

Some of us have had to learn bitterly that it can be better to go softly-softly when trying not to lose an audience. But for many of us, including Pearson, fidelity to wrath also comes as part of the character package. Diplomacy, needed as it is, also remains forever a form of untruth. It is hard to believe Pearson would manage to have the drive required for his positive reform offensive without the foil of opposition.

Yet this is an opposition whose anger, at first slow to wake up and get stirred into action, is itself partly his own creation. That is why he has them still partly on the back foot.

PETER SUTTON is an anthropologist at the University of Adelaide and the South Australian Museum. His most recent book is *The Politics of Suffering: Indigenous Australia and the End of the Liberal Consensus* (2009).

FRED CHANEY

I confess to experiencing moments of joy when reading Noel Pearson's essay. The opening pages made the rest of the piece irresistible reading. Like Noel, I found Lear's *Radical Hope* a beautiful book, which has remained in my thoughts. It captured for me the question that seems an urgent one for Aboriginal people: What does it mean to be Aboriginal in modern Australia? Before the culture of white settlers came to dominate, the meaning was clear. But the changes that occurred have made the old order, the old meaning, at best just one part of present Aboriginal identities. Crow chieftain Plenty Coups' statement – "*after this nothing happened*" – describing his life after the removal of the fundamental underpinnings of Crow culture – has to be seen in the context of his ongoing life, which lasted well beyond that time and involved distinguished service to the Crow nation. Lear's book is about what he could have meant by such a statement. But it seems clear that in terms of what was and what was no more, nothing could happen: the basis of Crow culture was gone. Lear's reconstruction of Plenty Coups' reasoning following a dream is that he was told that the traditional way of life was coming to an end and that, in these circumstances, "finding a way to flourish is the task for a new generation of Crow."

This seems to capture where European settlement has left Aboriginal people. It poses a key question that only Aboriginal people can answer: What does it mean to be Noongah or Adnamathana or any of the other Aboriginal identities in 2009 and beyond?

Noel offers "for discussion" what he describes in his essay as a question vital to Aboriginal people: "what it might mean to be a serious person and what it might mean to be a serious people ... when people are striving to maintain and to transmit to future generations their pre-modern cultures and languages in a modern, global world." His conclusion is that Aboriginal hope depends on how serious Aboriginal people become about the education of their people. Thus, the first fourteen pages of the essay pose a challenge for Aboriginal people. Much of the next 123 pages challenges educators and others to accept their responsibilities.

No writer is more at risk of selective quotation than Noel Pearson. That makes comment on his essay difficult. Here, as with his other writing, there is a risk of cherry-picking numerous quotable lines to confirm one's own views and ideological predilections. It is worth noting his reaffirmation of points made in earlier writings: his view that racism is a terrible ongoing burden and that dispossession has an ongoing impact is often overlooked by those quoting him on welfare reform. He also repeats another view of his: to believe one can advance more than one side in a dialectical tension is an illusion. This is the one point on which I seriously disagree with Noel. The issues facing Aboriginal Australians involve consideration of the impact of welfare, but, as Noel has eloquently argued elsewhere, they also involve the recognition of rights, including rights to land, and dealing with racism. Noel's passionate advocacy of welfare reform and tackling addiction has involved leaving the rights and racism agendas to others. It is for others, presumably governments, to deal with the totality of the agenda. I think that has been a mistake and has led to a distorted national debate because of Noel's pre-eminent position in that debate. His singular capacity to present a compelling case has led to the adoption of a false premise: that there is a single silver bullet available, welfare reform. In fact, it is only one critical piece of the jigsaw rather than the whole picture. Education is another key piece.

The chapter entitled "Groundhog Day" is utterly real. The endless recycling of policy pronouncements by governments, the total lack of memory – which means learning nothing from past successes or failures – and the critical point that policies never grapple with the challenges of implementation – all these things are described clearly and well. At a time when the commonwealth-led COAG arrangements involve clear government commitments to relevant outcomes, it remains true that delivery, rather than good intentions, is the problem. These are matters for other essays, but there is a vast gap between how commonwealth and state policies on remote communities are conceived and written up, and how they are delivered on the ground. We are therefore likely to follow what Noel describes as a predictable cycle. There will be public revelation and consternation about failure, followed by a new policy review, a new policy framework and a new commitment

– with Groundhog Day occurring every three to five years. Cast your mind back to the last COAG communiqué issued in Darwin along with the Productivity Commission's report on (the lack of) progress and the point is made. Noel's response then was, "Groundhog Day"; mine, "Words words words – I am so sick of words."

But the most powerful message of the essay is that if there is to be cultural survival, it has to be in a bicultural context. Survival under the old ways of transmitting culture is not possible because there is no mechanism in the old culture for dealing with the negative aspects of the settler culture, no way to control alcohol, no way to deal with the temptation to do nothing when welfare is available. A full Western education – education to understand and to be able to function in the post-Enlightenment world – is a necessity for Aboriginal survival. So is educating non-Indigenous students to value Indigenous culture – an aspect of reconciliation not dealt with in Noel's essay, but alluded to when he says that the achievement of socio-economic equality and biculturalism "will require a significant change of attitude in … the wider Australian public."

I came to the conclusion that education was the key through a more anecdotal and less analytical path than Noel. My final conversion to the belief that education is the critical factor – and by this I mean education in the dominant culture and in standard Australian English – came from observing the eastern goldfields of Western Australia. Seeing the degraded lives of fringe dwellers in Kalgoorlie, in from the Central Desert, seeing them on country in such different circumstances, made the point. It was captured by a senior man from the desert, who told me: "I worked in Kalgoorlie and have seen the way that our people coming into Kalgoorlie are fit to be nothing but fringe dwellers."

Having seen the lamentable lives and circumstances of so many of the people coming into centres such as Darwin (the long grassers), Alice Springs, Halls Creek and Kalgoorlie, many of whom have dignity born of solid commitment to country and culture when on their home ground, has led me to the conclusion that the old way *by itself* is no longer viable.

Some wonderful, strong Aboriginal people will deny this. But I think the evidence is irrefutable. What some of those people fear is that the sort of education Noel espouses will mean they cease to be Aboriginal. This very point was put to me in Alice Springs. In a way, that fear is correct – if being Aboriginal means being locked into a static cultural situation, required to be sufficient unto itself, yet without the old disciplines born of the necessity to survive by one's own efforts in a harsh environment. This fear underlines the relevance of the first eleven pages of the essay. It is necessary to re-imagine what it is to be Aboriginal in a world of store food, Toyotas, new media, gambling, drugs and so on. The numerous Aboriginal people I know who are bicultural are living examples of the possibility that one can be Aboriginal and confident in the dominant society. That possibility is not clear to people whose self-definition is as outsiders.

This brings to mind Peter Sutton's 2009 book *The Politics of Suffering* and the intersection of his and Noel's perspectives on culture. Valuing and nurturing culture in this way stimulates it to develop and survive in new circumstances. Perhaps this gives us somewhere to go with Peter's analysis of the destructive role of dislocated, devalued culture in remote communities today.

I was greatly reassured by Noel's references to reconciliation and its relevance to his central themes of education and culture. My sense is that Noel's essay and Peter's book both argue a case for reconciliation that is entirely consistent with our own case at Reconciliation Australia. They challenge the simplification of reconciliation to the "close the gap" mantra, explaining there is more to it than that, although improving the material circumstances of Aboriginal people is undoubtedly an essential goal.

As Noel puts it, the recognition that education (and all the gaps that are linked to it) is central to reconciliation is entirely justified, but so too is "the question of Aboriginal people's place within the Australian sovereign state." As Reconciliation Australia understands it, there's a gap that needs to be closed between us as fellow Australians. Building relationships that allow us to work together to improve Aboriginal people's life chances needs to happen on many levels, from the national level Noel describes to the personal level to which Peter Sutton gives priority.

Noel's discussion of how to teach Aboriginal children canvasses the conflicting conservative and leftist educational views. To me, Noel's case for educating disadvantaged children by using conservative approaches to pedagogy is convincing because it is in accord with my own life and experience and that of my wider family. It is consistent with my observation of

Aboriginal people educated conservatively (that is, they are numerate and literate and speak good English) now and in the past who have been able to live the lives they wish to lead. They are confident in two cultures and education has been the key to this.

We all see life through the prism of our own experience. Growing up in a public-housing area in Perth, I saw class and occupational differences. My teacher parents said they could leave us nothing, but their legacy would be a good education. Because my mother was Catholic and my non-Catholic father had been educated in Catholic schools by his Baptist mother, we all went to Catholic schools. I was acutely aware that they scrimped in order to pay our modest school fees. The parish school I attended was staffed by unpaid nuns – Brown Josephs – and those who could not pay did not. I was also aware from an early age that the Catholic schools were an exercise in lifting working-class kids into the middle class. It has been a successful exercise.

All of my many siblings and now their children have followed the path of education, enabling full involvement and engagement in Australian life. Whether it was business, law, medicine, politics, education, whatever we have aspired to be has been possible. In exactly the same way, I see Aboriginal people flourishing when they get a real educational opportunity. This goes beyond casual observation. Since 1997 a small private foundation I helped establish has worked with parents, schools and education authorities, mainly supported by the mining industry, to assist promising Aboriginal students to finish school *in their own communities*. The life possibilities for those who finish school are quite different from others in their cohort. They do not appear to be casting aside their Aboriginality in the process. Noel is right on the money in this regard. Truly equal education, a high standard of achievement in basic competencies, enables the disadvantaged, be they black, white or brindle, to take on the world on its terms. As Noel has pointed out, in this essay and elsewhere, high educational standards have not been destructive of Jewish identity.

Educationalists should feel some greater responsibility on reading this essay, but even more they should feel shame that, generations ago, Aboriginal people were getting a better education in literacy, numeracy and English from missionaries than many Aboriginal children are receiving today. When old men tell me that their children are "no good," I know it is not the children who have failed to learn; it is the teachers who have failed to teach.

It is a pity that Noel feels the need to challenge Chris Sarra and his approach to black pride as an educational tool. As a non-professional observer, I see much in common between Chris's approach and the No Excuses approach guiding Cape York educational reform. "Our culture is our strength" (Cape York) and "strong and smart" (Sarra) have much in common.

There may be something of an internal inconsistency in Noel's argument here. Is he suggesting that there is "Class" (Western education) and "Culture" (education in traditional languages etc.) and never the twain should meet? Or that while achievement in the latter depends on achievement in the former, the reverse is not the case? My view is that they are interconnected, just as pride in one's Aboriginal identity is connected with pride in culture.

If Aboriginal students aren't encouraged to take and *show* pride in their culture as a motivation for success, how can we encourage governments and the wider community to take pride in it, value it and invest in its survival, as Noel rightly asserts we must?

Most importantly, both Pearson and Sarra expect children to learn the full standard curriculum. Noel is correct to identify the common ground but does not emphasise what I think is the real difference between their approaches, with his focus on the use of income management as a tool, as against Sarra's belief that carrots are better than sticks in achieving parental and student involvement.

Comment could run on forever. The real point is to read the essay in full and for authorities to demand of their schools that classrooms be places where Aboriginal children are equipped for bicultural survival in the dominant culture, an outcome that is in all Australians' best interests.

FRED CHANEY is a former minister for Aboriginal Affairs and a research fellow in Aboriginal affairs, policy and administration at the University of Western Australia. He was a member of the National Native Title Tribunal and is currently a director of Reconciliation Australia.

Jane Caro

A relationship counsellor once described guilt to me as an absolutely useless emotion. It is the emotion you have, she said, when you feel the need to reassure yourself that you are – despite appearances to the contrary – a good person. We tend to feel guilt when we know we have behaved badly but have absolutely no intention of changing our behaviour, so, instead, we feel bad about whatever we have done to shore up our self-image. If we have really behaved badly, the counsellor argued, shame is a much better response, because shame feels so awful (nauseatingly, humiliatingly awful) that it is a real motivator to change. We can live with guilt, it seems, but not with shame.

With this in mind, I absolutely take Noel Pearson's point about much middle-class lefty rhetoric about Aboriginal Australians. I accept that many of us feel guilty about Aboriginal Australians and the shameful statistics in just about every area you care to mention regarding their life chances as compared to the rest of us. I also accept that much of our mealy-mouthed rhetoric about his people has been indulgent, designed to make us feel better, to shore up our own self-image, rather than actually do something concrete and effective about changing both the opportunities and outcomes for Aboriginal Australians.

I also accept that so far the education system in Australia has failed to improve very much for very many Indigenous people. As Pearson rightly points out, racism has had a lot to do with this lack of real progress, as has much of the well-meaning but ultimately self-serving rhetoric of earnest academics, reformers and pundits. But they have not stymied progress towards educational equality on their own.

According to Professor Barry McGaw, Australia has high-quality but relatively low-equity schooling compared with other high-quality countries. The troublesome "long tail" of under-achievement that dogs our every attempt to improve school performance keeps reminding us of this. Of course, there is no need to remind Noel Pearson that many Aboriginal school students can be found in that long tail. What is really tragic, however, is that, despite protestations to the contrary, Australia appears to be determinedly lengthening that tail, driving our most advantaged and most disadvantaged students even farther apart. We are doing this by developing a two-tiered education system comprising a well-resourced, partly publicly funded, fee-charging private-school sector for the better-off or the talented, and an ever less well-resourced, publicly funded sector for the rest.

The results of this thirty-year trend have been devastating for educational equality and for disadvantaged students of all kinds, including Aboriginal kids. In 1996, according to researcher Barbara Preston, there were thirteen students from low-income families to every ten students from high-income families in the playgrounds of our public high schools. By 2006, that had risen to sixteen low-income students to every ten high-income students. To put that another way, 26 per cent of students in independent schools are from high-income households, compared to 16 per cent at Catholic schools and a dwindling (and terrifying) 8 per cent at government schools.

Pearson hardly mentions public and private schooling in his essay except to make the following point: "If I have learned anything about public education, it is that it is thoroughly class-sensitive in its provisioning. What it provides to middle-class kids at Edge Hill in Cairns is palpably different to what it provides at Cairns West." He is, of course, right to the extent that public schools still reflect the community they serve. (Though, if Preston's figures are correct, then almost all public schools now enrol the poorest children in their area, even if their poverty is only relative.) But the relative inequality of public schools is no reason for governments and policy-makers to throw up their hands in despair and actively encourage the exit of the middle class from public education altogether. In wealthy metropolitan areas, Sydney's eastern suburbs for example, this separation of wealthier citizens from public education has reached extremes. There are only three public high schools left in Sydney's prosperous east, and two of them are single-sex. It is seriously worrying when not just the school but the school systems our children attend are predicated on the economic background or class aspirations of their parents. The only schools that are open to all are rapidly losing their middle-class families.

This matters because our most advantaged, influential and articulate citizens have less and less personally invested in the fortunes of the schooling system that educates more and more of our poorest and neediest children, including 88 per cent of Aboriginal children. Their energies, loyalties and abilities go into private education instead. It also matters because of the inevitable message it sends kids in public schools, no matter what colour their skin is. The message they receive is that they are less valuable, less desirable and less will be expected of them. Plucking a few fortunate kids from their local schools and exposing them to the heady world of the wealthy may help those lucky individuals, but it does nothing to help educational equality in this country and probably actively harms it.

This wholesale flight by better-off families from our public-education system is explained as the consequence of parental choice. Some blame what they see as "failing" public schools for driving those parents who can, to jump ship; others blame the compounding effect over decades of deliberate government policy, ideologically driven funding and an increasingly anxious population of middle-class parents with fewer children and much more money to spend on them. One thing over which there can be no dispute, however, is that parental choice is why some teachers and principals are starting to talk about an emerging "de facto apartheid" in our schooling system. In a recent survey, public-school principals expressed their concern about an increasing concentration of Indigenous kids in public schools and a corresponding flight of white kids to other schools, especially in rural areas.

Parental choice in some parts of Australia seems to mean choosing not to have your kid sit next to a black kid. In some parts of our major cities, it means choosing not to have your kid sit next to a kid in a hijab. Few admit to this as being part of the motivation behind their choice, although some of the less sophisticated are prepared to claim that private schools educate – and I quote – "a nicer class of kiddy." Most will make solemn – if ignorant – claims about private schools having better teachers and a better curriculum, even though all teachers are trained in the same unis in the same pedagogy that Pearson criticises so vigorously in his essay, and the curriculum is the same across public and private schools in all states of Australia. Some will admit to seeking better discipline, which I believe basically means that parents know naughty kids are more easily excluded from private schools than public ones.

Parental choice is applauded most by those who are considered to be on the right of the political divide, but make no mistake: middle-class lefties (while feeling suitably guilty about choosing a private school) also take full advantage of it.

However, I want to avoid (as much as I can) the terms "Left" and "Right" in my response to Pearson's essay. I believe the attempt to transplant the economic and ideological ideas that have formed our sense of the Left and Right wings of politics carries much of the responsibility for our growing educational inequality. The market-driven ideas of capital and labour, and of the individual versus the collective, have caused much of the damage. Those who believe that competition and a free market can solve every conceivable problem are blind to the damage market forces are doing to the educational opportunities of our most disadvantaged children, and those who believe the interests of the collective should always triumph over those of the individual are blind to the hopes and fears of real, living, breathing human parents.

The British philosopher Stephen Law in his book *The War for Children's Minds* redraws the battlelines by demonstrating that rather than Left or Right, the real battle in education is between the authoritarians and the liberals.

What is fascinating about his redefinition is that it reveals how selectively both sides of the educational divide apply their particular philosophies. After all, parental choice looks very much like a liberal value – every individual parent should have the right to choose the best way to educate their children (if they can afford it, of course). Conversely, the pleas of those of us horrified by the demise of public education are often decried as authoritarian – wanting to force every family into the same, monolithic state-controlled mould. Yet, when it comes to what goes on in the classroom, each side neatly flips on its head. The pundits who are vociferous in their defence of parental choice often applaud an authoritarian pedagogy, while defenders of public education are often much more comfortable with a more liberal approach.

Pearson's essay, it seems to me – while he never uses the term – is about the effectiveness of an authoritarian approach to pedagogy, particularly for disadvantaged children and particularly for Aboriginal children. Indeed, the very names of the programs he extols indicate as much: "No Excuses," "Direct Instruction," "Prescriptive Teaching," even "Knowledge Is Power." As I am neither an Indigenous Australian nor an educator, I bow to his greater knowledge and understanding of what works inside a classroom for children who have been born and brought up in vastly different circumstances from my own. I remain bewildered, however, by his vociferous support for the phonics side of what I see as a phoney war between phonics and whole-language approaches to teaching children to read. It has never seemed to me that the phonics and whole-language approaches are mutually exclusive and I believe that most sensible classroom teachers agree with me. They read children stories (whole language), stick the names of things around the classroom (whole language) and help beginning readers to sound out the words (phonics). Surely we should ban neither and encourage both. Why must it be the carrot or the stick – why not a little of both, judiciously and appropriately applied?

Nevertheless, I am in awe of Pearson's dedication and determination to change the educational outcomes for the Indigenous children of Cape York. More strength to his arms, if the levers he pulls bring about favourable results.

What concerns me still, however, is the long-term future of educational equality in Australia. While a more authoritarian approach to pedagogy may help in some classrooms, the increasing socio-economic educational apartheid in our playgrounds cannot bode well. The elephant in the room in Australia's education system is that we have one group of publicly funded schools with all the rights (the right to choose who they will or won't educate, the right to choose where they will build schools, the right to charge whatever fees they deem appropriate, the right to expel the troublesome or the low-achieving) and another group of publicly funded schools with all the responsibilities – particularly when it comes to educating all Australian children, whoever they are, wherever they live, no matter what difficulties they bring through the school gate. And as long as that's how we design our education provision, we will never have any hope of achieving improvements in our long-term educational equality.

My radical hope is a curiously old-fashioned one. I hope that one day all our children, regardless of who their parents are, will have access to well-funded, inclusive schools. That the educational resources available to children in our most socially disadvantaged areas will be as good as, if not better than, those available to children who live in wealthier areas. I hope that our children will go to school and not just learn the curriculum but also that there are as many ways to live a good life as there are people living lives. But, most of all, I hope that the schools that are open to all children and that do not charge fees are regarded as the best, not just in the country, but in the world.

And I will feel not guilt but shame until they are.

JANE CARO is the co-author, with Chris Bonnor, of *The Stupid Country: How Australia Is Dismantling Public Education* (2007).

Andrew Leigh

In an international survey, a random sample of Australians and Americans were asked which factors were important to getting ahead in life. On most questions, the two groups concurred. But asked about education, nine out of ten Americans rated it "essential" or "very important," compared with just seven out of ten Australians. Subsequent research by the Australian National University's Youth in Focus team suggests that Australian income-support recipients are even less likely to believe that education matters.

Perhaps it should not be surprising that education is regarded as less important in the Lucky Country. By the 1940s, the typical American student had finished Year 12. It was not until the mid-1980s that the same could be said of young Australians. Today, about one in four Australian students still fails to complete high school. When US politicians speak to schoolchildren in low-income areas, they deliver the same message that they give their own children: study hard, finish school and go on to university if you can. When Australian politicians deliver speeches to young people in working-class neighbourhoods, they are much less likely to stress the value of formal education.

In this context, Noel Pearson's call for education to be at

the core of Indigenous policy is refreshingly direct. It is not merely about increasing the quantity of education that Indigenous people receive, but also about raising the quality of that education. It asks more of government (particularly through raising teacher quality) but also of parents and students (in Pearson's words, "Aboriginal Australians must become a serious people").

Does school quality really matter? One of the strongest pieces of evidence on this point is that the black–white test-score gap widens over the lifecycle. According to the work that I have done with my colleague Xiaodong Gong, the typical Indigenous child starts school one year behind their non-Indigenous classmates. By the time they finish primary school, Indigenous children are two years behind. Paradoxically, I think this is good news for reformers, since schools are more amenable to policy intervention than families. Half the test-score gap can be closed simply by ensuring that Indigenous children learn at the same rate as non-Indigenous children while they are at school.

Pearson's essay touches on many of the critical issues for improving schools, not just in Indigenous communities but across the nation. He recollects a "hugely beneficial" fifth-grade teacher who had a major educational impact, yet whose name he can no longer recall. This emphasises that when it comes to effectiveness in the classroom, we should beware of formulas for successful teaching. Pearson also points out that instructional approaches and teacher quality are intimately related: the more talented the teacher, the more freedom the curriculum can allow them. He might have noted that the same is true of remuneration and dismissal: the case for merit pay would be weaker if it was easier to remove under-performing teachers.

Teaching disadvantaged children is perhaps the most important job in Australia. Yet we lack the innovative policies that would help to ensure that the most talented teachers are drawn to the most disadvantaged schools. The same reluctance characterises interventions to boost participation and performance. Where new policies have been trialled, it is generally in an ad hoc manner, leaving others uncertain about the efficacy of particular policies.

Recognising this, Pearson writes about the need for education policy-makers to rely more upon data and less on ideology. Discussing teaching methods, he cites the willing-ness of researchers to ignore Siegfried Engelmann's Direct Instruction approach, despite many rigorous studies backing it up. Pearson is right to point out the travesty of ignoring good evidence. But in most cases, we simply do not have high-quality evidence about what works.

To build the evidence base, it will be necessary for policy-makers to run the kinds of scientifically rigorous experi-ments that are commonplace in the medical literature. With a randomised experiment, you can be confident that differ-ences between the treatment and control groups are truly causal. Without randomisation, we are usually left unsure whether changes in the treatment population are due to the policy or would have occurred anyway.

Randomised experiments would be a radical step in Indigenous policy. Some will contend that it is unethical to decide which individual gets a treatment based on the toss of a coin. Others will argue that local knowledge should determine which policies are implemented. Under this view, self-determination precludes randomised evaluation.

Yet randomised policy trials are simply the logical extension of Pearson's call for evidence over ideology. If the principles of the Enlightenment are to guide Indigenous education policies (as he advocates), then we need to begin putting some of our theories to the test. And the most rigorous test around is the randomised policy trial.

Of course, we already do this in Indigenous health policy. When it comes to assessing the effectiveness of a diabetes drug for Indigenous Australians, scientists and politicians would agree that it should be evaluated using a randomised control group. By tossing a coin, we ensure that the treatment group (for whom the coin came up heads) are as similar as possible to the control group (for whom the coin came up tails). And while we might conduct some focus groups on the side, the ultimate test would be effectiveness: did the new drug do a better job of treating the disease?

In the same vein, we should be willing to run experiments in Indigenous education: judging reforms on results, not just theory. Are we better off spending money on smaller classes or higher teacher salaries? Could we boost attendance by paying all Indigenous children $20 a week to show up to school? Do Indigenous children learn better from Indigenous teachers? Do children benefit more from longer school years or longer school days? Do nutrition programs have an educational pay-off? Does Direct Instruction raise both test scores and self-esteem for Indigenous Australian students? Could merit pay improve student learning, or would it just sow divisiveness in the staffroom? So far as I am aware, we have no rigorous randomised evidence from Australia on any of these interventions.

In international development, the large-scale adoption of randomised trials has been driven by the recognition that despite $2.5 trillion of foreign aid over the past half-century, many developing nations remain desperately poor. In the words of William Easterly, "planners" (with grand visions about how to end poverty) now need to be replaced by "searchers" (who rigorously test small-scale interventions). In Indigenous policy, most sensible policy-makers quietly agree that many of our policies are ineffective. Yet the policy debates are still dominated by planners, with their overarching theories. The evidence base remains paper-thin.

One of the things randomised trials have taught us is that impressive-sounding programs can flop. To take just one example, its boosters often argue that Neighbourhood Watch reduces crime. Going on theory alone, it is easy to tell compelling stories about how the program *should* be effective. Indeed, low-quality evaluations (using matched control groups, say) suggest that the program works. Yet randomised trials almost invariably find that Neighbourhood Watch does nothing to cut crime. Raise the evidence bar and the answer changes.

A move from ideology to empirics (from planning to searching, in Easterly's language) would require a good deal more modesty from policy-makers. Rather than judging programs based on case studies and theory, we could use the same rigour that we apply to new pharmaceuticals. Despite ideological battles over particular Indigenous policies, there is broad agreement over the "Closing the Gaps" targets. So why not rigorously assess each new Indigenous intervention according to whether or not it can be proven to help close one or more of the gaps?

The urgency of the problem should not be an excuse for lowering the evidence bar. The federal government would never have funded this year's nationwide rollout of swine-flu vaccine without seeing the results of randomised clinical trials. Yet the 2007 intervention was implemented across the Northern Territory with zero randomised evidence. If we want to know the causal impact of banning pornography, quarantining welfare or scrapping CDEP, a handful of randomised trials would tell us more than overblown rhetoric and angry accusations ever could.

Once we raise the evidence bar in Indigenous education, we may look back and wonder how we ever settled for less. In the United States, a strong advocate of randomised trials in education is Roland Fryer, the youngest African-American ever to become a full professor at Harvard. In a 2008 interview, he told the *New York Times*: "If the doctor said to you, 'You have a cold; here are three pills my buddy in Charlotte uses and he says they work,' you would run out and find another doctor. Somehow, in education, that approach is OK."

Fryer is currently running a series of randomised experiments across Chicago, New York and Washington D.C., evaluating interventions such as high-quality charter schools and paying students who receive good grades. The essence of his approach is humility in the face of data. As he puts it: "We will have the willingness to try new things and be wrong – the type of humbleness to say, 'I have no idea whether this will work, but I'm going to try.'"

There are many proposals to love in Pearson's eloquent essay. But can we meld his careful ideas and deep experience with Fryer's scientific rigour? Or, to put it another way, Pearson may well be right, but is he willing to be wrong?

ANDREW LEIGH is the federal member for Fraser in the ACT. Before entering politics, he was a professor of economics at the Australian National University.

NOEL PEARSON: *Reply*

I have been working with colleagues and community leaders on a proposal to develop No Excuses schools in remote communities in Cape York Peninsula. Our proposition to the commonwealth and Queensland governments is to establish a Cape York Aboriginal Australian Academy, a specialist kindergarten to Year 7 remote-schools provider which will have legislative delegation within the Queensland public school system to provide education where Indigenous parent communities support this alternative. Our proposed reform model will strengthen public education. While there are many features that differ from existing provisioning, most of these have a strong resonance with prevalent thinking about educational reform.

If any point is fundamental to our academy proposal, it is its governance. We are seeking the necessary delegation of autonomy to enable an independent board to provide the direction and support to the educators in the communities whom we will rely upon to deliver our vision. We want to replace governance by the system with governance by a group of people who see their role as enabling and assisting the educators to create not just a school or a group of schools, but a high-quality and lasting institution. Institutions take time to build, but when they have been established they have momentum and longevity that outlast the changing of personnel. Institutions have those intangible things – values, culture, traditions, expectations, pride, attachment and so on – which can make success self-perpetuating and sustainable over time.

The problem with small schools generally, and with remote communities in particular, is that the fast turnover of teaching personnel (the three-year average in Cape York is about as good as we can expect) and of school leadership – and the absence of any formal leadership engagement of Aboriginal people – means that it is impossible to develop an institution that embeds and sustains a culture of high expectations and no excuses. There have been many times when schools served by great teachers or great school leaders have shown great promise – but you're back to square one when the next leader comes along.

As well as remoteness, the small scale of these schools makes the development of a high-quality institution almost impossible because of the constant flux. The answer is to create networks of grouped schools where an institutional identity can capture both a local and a wider network identity – the creation of state colleges in Weipa in Cape York Peninsula and Thursday Island in Torres Strait has gone a long way towards this.

I believe that the academy we have proposed will only work if I and other like-minded people who are passionate and competent are able to mandate the ethos and culture of the kind of institution that is needed: this is what is so hard to achieve with traditional public schooling, particularly at the scale with which we are dealing. I am not saying that a No Excuses, Best of Both Worlds philosophy is the only possible kind of school ethos and approach that can work. Educators with different views, such as Chris Sarra, should also be given the autonomy to chart Indigenous education-reform programs within the public·education system.

The intended structure of the academy was only briefly and indirectly described in my *Quarterly Essay*. The public presentation of our plan, to which the correspondents did not have access, has clarified some issues that are of concern to them. For example, we do not believe we can reform remote education as an "autonomous field" in isolation from "inter-related areas" such as health, housing and so on, as Christine Nicholls suspected was the case. Reform of education supply is very much an integral part of a comprehensive development agenda.

However, most of the comments in the rich harvest of correspondence have stimulated me to grapple further with fundamental questions. The correspondents raised issues that fall into two broad categories. First, Indigenous educational failure may be seen as our most extreme example of social disadvantage, without any particular regard paid to the larger issue of Indigenous Australians' place in our nation. Questions of culture and self-determination may be relevant to this kind of discussion, but fundamentally Aboriginal reconciliation is defined as closing the social and economic gap. The objective of policy is not to institute further recognition of the special status of Indigenous Australians, and no assumption is made that such recognition is conducive to educational advancement. The question is simply what sets Indigenous children on a life trajectory of successful schooling, tertiary study and prosperity.

Second, education may be viewed from the point of view of cultural self-determination and preservation of Indigenous Australian culture.

Most correspondents apply both perspectives. The only correspondent who discusses my essay purely from the former angle is Andrew Leigh. He correctly observes that "teaching disadvantaged children is perhaps the most important job in Australia" and he appears to view Indigenous education solely as an issue of removing educational disadvantage. The question Leigh implicitly asks is, "How do we find out which policies will lift Indigenous academic achievement to main-stream standards?" He reads my suggestion that Aboriginal Australians have a serious discussion about what it might mean to be "a serious people" as an exhortation to Aboriginal parents to become engaged in their children's education and to Aboriginal students to work harder – which is correct, but not the whole point I tried to make.

Nonetheless, Leigh's response is important because he insists that "the urgency of the problem should not be an excuse for lowering the evidence bar." The only evidence that will ultimately be of any value, Leigh argues, is randomised trials. Leigh is probably Australia's most consistent advocate of rigorous randomised trials as the sole meaningful basis for evidence-based policy. Because of the absence of systematic formulation and trialling of conceivable policies, we "do not have high-quality evidence about what works," and the range of policies that have been tried is limited.

Leigh perceptively observes that "self-determination precludes randomised evaluation." The establishment of our academy proposal will depend on an active choice by local parent communities and elected leaders.

The comments by Peter Shergold (and Jane Caro's plea for educational equality in Australia) are likewise mainly concerned with bridging "the appalling chasm of disadvantage." Shergold challenges my assertion that bureaucracies have no memory. Many individual public servants indeed remember the lack of substance behind so much vainglorious political rhetoric, Shergold writes. But he goes on to concede that the experience of public servants "too often feeds hardnosed cynicism."

I did not mean to imply that all public servants with firsthand experience suffer from amnesia when I asserted that governments and bureaucracies have no memory – I said that true memory entails moral responsibility, which is the opposite of cynicism.

Christine Nicholls, who lived and worked for many years as an educator and school principal in a remote community where an Aboriginal language is still the first language, is naturally more engaged in her discussion of the preservation of Australia's Aboriginal cultures as a goal in its own right – an indispensable element of reconciliation. Nicholls writes that my "aspiration to hold on to Aboriginal knowledge and cultural practices, languages and traditions, some of which are experiencing severe strain, is of the utmost importance" and supports my "insistence that governments, as well as individuals, have critically important responsibilities in this respect." Nicholls notes that Australia's remaining Aboriginal languages are in urgent need of legislative protection.

However, Nicholls' advocacy for new policies for the survival of Australia's national minorities is no more passionate than could be expected from an educator and academic with her experience and research interests. The most important reaction to my essay has come from the most culturally conservative quarters.

Tony Abbott concludes that the importance of a "standard academic education" and "the need for Aboriginal people to be able to participate in the broader economy on their merits" are not the main points of my essay. "Effective participation in wider society," Abbott writes, "is more a by-product of the education that [Pearson] wants for young Aborigines; it's not the main objective."

That is perhaps overstating it. Man cannot live by bread alone, but he does need bread, and in the modern world the broader economy is where he'll earn it. But Abbott recognises that, even though my texts (including my *Quarterly Essay*) are often perceived to mainly challenge the Left, the bigger challenge may well be reserved for the Right.

The political Right will probably be divided on this challenge. Those on the culturally shallow Right, whose conservatism does not extend far beyond simple advocacy for economic liberalism, will not instinctively grasp, as Abbott does, that the challenge is "to accept that biculturalism, at least for Aboriginal people, is a worthy object of Australian government policy and is worth paying for."

Christopher Pearson responded to my *Quarterly Essay* in the *Weekend Australian* on 31 October 2009 with words similar to Abbott's:

> Noel Pearson ... invokes the example of Jews and their remarkable successes in the fields of both mainstream academic instruction and maintenance of a distinctive culture. He thinks that without the active support of state and private schools, combined with higher overall standards and sustained formal instruction in Aboriginal languages and traditions, indigenous high cultures will vanish.
>
> If there were one priority in national cultural policy on which most of us could wholeheartedly agree, surely this is it ... If we want there to be a rising generation fluent in Pitjantjatjara and the other main endangered language groups – apart from geriatrics and European linguists – we must encourage and reward them and the people who train them.
>
> Creole or children's versions of Aboriginal languages are no more suitable to ceremony or the recitation of Dreaming stories than are colloquial English or play-ground slang to the articulation of the meta-narratives of the West. Whether Aboriginal religions can be re-invigorated, as opposed to indigenous cultures in a more general sense, remains to be seen. But turning a blind eye to an existing education system that deprives indigenous

kids of an adequate grounding in either the basics of ordinary education or their own cultures is philistinism on a grand scale.

Christopher Pearson's article convinces me that Tony Abbott's principled response to my essay is not necessarily unrepresentative of conservative Australian thinking and a mere product of Abbott's close association with Cape York reform projects and his friendship with my colleagues and myself (or, for that matter, of his friendship with Christopher Pearson). A common chord is struck with conservatives.

The explanation is, of course, that serious conservatives such as Abbott and Pearson understand the existential importance of "meta-narratives" and of languages, literatures and spiritual traditions for their own sake in a way that well-intentioned but culturally modernist supporters of Aboriginal people do not, be they from the right-of-centre, left-liberal or progressive bands of the political spectrum.

Christopher Pearson and Tony Abbott intuitively understand that Aboriginal Australians' languages and traditions are at the spiritual centre of our nation and that they are not only for Aboriginal Australians. Furthermore, they realise that the cathedral is on fire.

Abbott suspects that I underestimate the magnitude of the task of maintaining, revitalising and reviving Australia's own culture. I do not. On the contrary, I suspect that the public does not understand the grave problems of Aboriginal languages and traditions as they are now, including those languages and traditions that are believed to be relatively intact. There needs to be a rapid development of the material and institutional infrastructure supporting our languages and cultures. The number of non-Indigenous Australians competent in our languages and cultures needs to increase by several orders of magnitude within the next few years. What needs to be done needs to be the subject of a separate discussion.

In my Judith Wright Lecture in 2004, I concluded that:

The political truism that only Nixon could go to China is pertinent here. Only a highly conservative leader, one who enjoys the confidence of the most conservative sections of the national community – those in rural and regional Australia – will be able to lead the country to an appropriate resolution of these issues. It will take a prime minister in the mould of Tony Abbott to lead the nation to settle the "unfinished business" between settler Australians and the other people who are members of this nation: the Indigenous people.

In that speech I was mainly (but, of course, not exclusively) referring to a national agreement that would settle land issues, economic and social issues and constitutional recognition of Indigenous Australians. The names might change, but the political analysis stands.

I regret that I cannot respond to all issues raised by the correspondents. Fred Chaney's deeply personal text demonstrates that a readiness to participate in the maintenance and development of Australia's cultures is perhaps more widespread than I thought.

AFTERWORD

I started writing *Radical Hope* after my colleagues and I completed a business plan for the establishment of a new primary-school provider: the Cape York Aboriginal Australian Academy. The Academy represented the culmination of policy reform thinking and trials undertaken by Cape York Partnerships based in Cairns over the best part of the previous decade.

I showed our plan to federal minister Jenny Macklin, who became our champion and arranged a meeting with the Queensland premier, Anna Bligh. The then education minister, Julia Gillard, had given significant funding to the states and territories on condition that the state pursue specified reforms. Macklin and Gillard saw our Academy as a reform that fitted with the Commonwealth's reform intentions.

Anna Bligh agreed and set the wheels in motion. It was late in 2009, and there were bureaucratic hurdles to overcome. The Queensland education department's research unit examined the business plan, and particularly our intention to use the programs from the United States developed by Siegfried Engelmann from the National Institute for Direct Instruction. It endorsed our proposed program as supported by a strong evidence base in the literature.

After a bureaucratic tussle, we came to an agreement with the Queensland government on Christmas Eve 2009, giving us less than a month to be ready to start up our Academy in the Cape York communities of Aurukun (240 students) and Coen (fifty students).

There are four components to our program: Class, Club, Culture and Community.

The Class program is about literacy and numeracy, and we utilise full-immersion Direct Instruction programs, running from 8.30 a.m. to 2.30 p.m. Our partners from NIFDI in the United States oversee the implementation of D.I. by sending experienced educators out to train the teachers in the delivery of the programs and provide coaching and professional-development support through the course of the year.

Children are tested at the beginning and placed in groups according to their current ability levels. In the case of Aurukun a vast number of the students were reading at kindergarten level, so that's where we started with them. There is no use in trying to teach a Year 5 student at her age level when she is at Year 2 or kindergarten level: you have to work at a level where students can achieve success and build momentum and enthusiasm for accelerated learning so that they catch up over time.

The whole school is involved in D.I. – all of the teachers and all of the students. The time allocated for instruction is jealously guarded as the most precious resource.

The D.I. programs are remarkable. The students are tested for mastery every five to ten lessons. The programs ensure that students have achieved 90 per cent mastery of the material before they move on. New material is incrementally added while old material is reinforced systematically.

Geoff Higham, the Aurukun principal, wrote to me:

Each Tuesday morning at 7.00 a.m., [Aurukun curriculum coordinator] Colleen Page and I join [NIFDI project directors] Vicki Vachon, Claudia McKnight and [Academy instructional coach] Lizzy Fuller in a trans-Pacific teleconference to analyse and assess the individual efforts of each teacher and his/her classes re the implementation of D.I. As each teacher and pupil comes under the microscope, it is easy to see why Direct Instruction cannot but succeed if given the right support. The passionate yet objective and professional manner in which the data is presented and dissected eliminates personality, philosophy and preference from the process and brings forth the simple reality of performance. Ultimately, every gesture and word can be evaluated as to its effectiveness. Only the most skilful manipulation of results could escape quick detection under this system and, even then, eventual and relatively rapid exposure would be inevitable.

For someone like me who has been around the ridges of social structures and programs for some time now, the consistency and rigour that the Americans bring to the implementation of the D.I. programs is extraordinary. The teleconferences happen rain, hail or shine. There are no excuses for anything.

The second learning domain is called Club, where we seek to offer music, sport and other extracurricular activities such as the web-based Mathletics program. Our aspiration is to provide these enrichment opportunities so that we lessen the opportunity gap between our students and middle-class children who receive what the American sociologist Annette Lareau calls "concerted cultivation" from their parents out of school hours. So we have burgeoning partnerships with the Australian Football League and Tennis Australia to provide high-quality programs to kids in remote communities.

We want children in remote primary schools not to miss out on anything that might foreclose their future possibilities. For example, we want students to have the opportunity to read music and learn to play an instrument during their primary schooling; otherwise, a future pathway in music will be closed to them. Two items that remain on my aspirational list are to offer a foreign language and to establish a Shakespeare drama club.

The third learning domain is called Culture, which includes the teaching of the local Aboriginal Australian language.

Club and Culture require additional teachers to specialise in music, sport and Australian languages, and they require a full eight-hour school day. The extended school day is voluntary and is subject to parents' enrolment of their children; almost all of the children are enrolled.

The learning program is supported by a Community program, which involves case management of school attendance and readiness; a food program, which provides meals during the day; and a facility for families to put funds aside for their children's educational expenses, called Student Education Trusts (SETs). At any one time an average of $1500 is accumulated in each of these accounts and is available to pay for uniforms, books, student excursions and, according to the choices made by parents, laptop computers. Across the four communities that have established SETs, more than a million dollars has accumulated in these trusts simply by parents and relatives setting aside a reasonable deduction from their income on a weekly basis so as to cater to their children's educational needs. SETs are voluntary, there is no government subsidy, and the facility is universally supported by parents. Perhaps the most gratifying expenditures out of these SETs have in recent years been students paying for their high-school graduation dresses at whatever boarding school they are attending down south.

The introduction of the Academy and the D.I. programs last year was fraught. Having done the deal with the Queensland government on the Christmas Eve prior, there had been no chance to talk to the existing teachers and principals about the reforms that we intended to introduce, and to give them the opportunity to decide whether they wished to continue. We wanted to make sure the teachers were given a choice to teach at the Academy, but the tangled bureaucratic process made it impossible.

So there were ructions. With some of the teachers. With the principals. With some parents and community members. And with the local media. The local paper, the *Cairns Post*, seized upon controversies in the first weeks, including a front-page beat-up about how children at our schools were required to learn the "Star-Spangled Banner." It was nonsense. There was an attempt in the early stages for detractors to seize upon the Americanisms in the D.I. materials (the simple solution is for the teachers to make the conversions from imperial measurements to SI (metric) units, change "color" to "colour," and so on), as if these were a great evil in the program. There was quite a bit of manufactured trouble generated by detractors.

With the natural difficulties associated with acclimatising teachers and their students to a new and very much more demanding program, and dealing with the legacy of long-standing problems of behaviour management in the schools – particularly at Aurukun – the first term of 2010 was difficult. I did not know how we would go.

It was like standing in the middle of a cyclone. At a public meeting with parents in Coen I assured them that my own children were receiving D.I. at home.

But order was emerging from the chaos. The teachers were getting on top of the program; the students started to feel some success from their learning; everybody had their roles and knew what they had to do. The time-out room, which had peaked with dozens of kids, now had only a handful. The teacher supervising behaviour management would soon return to classroom teaching.

Towards the end of the first term, before Easter, the storm passed and the schools started humming. Geoff Higham wrote to me:

Walking around the Aurukun campus on Holy Thursday morning left me with a feeling of real contentment. The children in the lower classes had been invited to the Child

Care Centre for the annual Easter Hat Parade and, understandably, the Prep children were jumping about, sporting their rabbit ears in anticipation of the coming event. However, every other class from Grade One through to our secondary cohort was engaged in Direct Instruction as usual. I doubt whether any other government school in the state could boast such dedication to teaching and learning on the last day of term.

The teachers, school leaders and staff of the Academy worked hard for the rest of the year, and the schools just kept lifting and lifting. Anyone who knows anything about schools will know that there is no shortage of reversals and crises, but the trend was always upwards.

At the end of the first year I was bold enough to assert that while one of our schools would have been a contender for the title of Australia's most disadvantaged school (all of the nominees for which would come from remote Indigenous communities), both of our schools were contenders for the top tier of Indigenous schools. This is not a claim about where they are at (Aurukun, in particular, is starting from way behind in the race, as evidenced by the fact that the great majority of the primary-school students were found to be at kindergarten level for reading at the beginning), but about where they are heading. They have become highly coherent schools where effective teaching of the children is the apex of all endeavours and activities.

Direct Instruction, by supplying the substance of the relationship between the teachers and their students, provides a complete logic to the organisation and operation of these two schools. When the teacher delivers effective instruction, the student experiences learning success, and when the student tastes learning success, the student's behaviour becomes good, and when the student's behaviour becomes good, the virtuous circle starts turning. And then on some days, Geoff Higham tells me, he hears it hum.

There are daily challenges and there is a mountain in front of us. But the children are unmistakably on the climb.

In the second half of last year community leaders and parents from my home town, Hope Vale, started talking about their interest in Direct Instruction for their school. Not wanting to provoke political opposition I had decided to leave it to the people of my home community to take responsibility and exercise their own leadership for the education of their children.

A group of parents and members of the Hope Vale Council travelled to Aurukun and Coen and saw the Academy in practice. They talked to fellow leaders, teachers and the people from NIFDI. They decided to ask the Americans and our Academy people to come and talk about introducing Direct Instruction.

They then wrote to the government. There was opposition from some parts of the bureaucracy, but Premier Anna Bligh gave the go-ahead in December 2010.

Once again there was a mad scramble over the Christmas holidays to get ready for a January start, and the Hope Vale campus of the Cape York Aboriginal Australian Academy is now underway.

And while this happens, my correspondent in Aurukun, Geoff Higham, writes to me two weeks into the second year:

The overall atmosphere of the school presents itself as revolutionary compared with what could be felt at this time last year. The children are now being escorted to class quietly and in straight lines, every classroom is a place of effective teaching and learning and the staff are more positive, better presented and, overall, much happier.

We are very pleased with the current attendance figures. Even taking into account the difficulties re regular attendance in our secondary school; without the assistance of case management, I'm told that the overall attendance figures are hovering around the 75 per cent mark which, although not up to Tony Abbott's 100 per cent goal, is a long way ahead of the reality of what was happening in this school before the advent of Direct Instruction.

Nevertheless, there are still problems. Our sustained efforts to ensure that all children are behaving appropriately in class has brought some recalcitrants out of the woodwork and we are following through with a series of corrective strategies in order to bring them back into the fold. As one would expect, we are having varying rates of success.

His conclusion:

There is currently no class in the school that is failing. Unquestionably, the new teachers are advancing at individual rates and the returning teachers still have room for improvement but the consistency of pedagogy observable throughout the school is markedly more even than that which was observed at the end of last year. I continue to be impressed with the quality, dedication and rapid adaptation of the new teachers to the Direct Instruction model.

At present, I must admit that I have no complaints at all. Naturally, things are not perfect. There are a couple of teachers who are finding it difficult to cope with classes where there is a concentration of difficult children and we are doing everything in our power to support those teachers. Nevertheless, we don't appear to be dealing with any issues that we can't cope with. Extra help in the classrooms is what we need and once the Day 8 figures are finalised [the number of students attending on the eighth day determines resource allocation] we'll know if we have access to funds to employ any more teachers' aides, but until that time comes we'll continue to do the best we can with the personnel available. It's a school and, like in any other school, there are and always will be occasions when we have to battle against the odds.

Nevertheless, the overall perception is definitely that all's well on the Class front.

I wrote in 2009 that our hope depends on education: "Radical hope for the future of Aboriginal Australia ... will require the bringing together of the Enlightenment and Aboriginal

Australian culture … The education of our children in both traditions … is … fundamental to this hope."

On Cape York Peninsula we have shown that our vision is feasible: that all Aboriginal Australian children, even those in remote areas, can have a primary education that enables them to proceed to quality secondary and tertiary education, and take their place in the national and global communities.

So our hope is being fulfilled, then? I suspect that my buoyant assessment of the achievements of educators, students and parents on Cape York Peninsula since 2009 will be partly misunderstood by those who support me and my colleagues.

To explain this I need to revisit the first point I made in *Radical Hope*. Quoting Jonathan Lear, I said that what makes the hope – of a people who have lost their old world – *radical* is that "it is directed towards a future goodness that transcends the current ability to understand what it is. Radical hope anticipates a good for which those who have the hope as yet lack the appropriate concepts with which to understand it."

"Closing the Gap" in education, and Aboriginal Australians' internalisation of the Enlightenment, are necessary for my people to take their rightful place in the national and global communities. But those things don't transcend our current understanding.

To see what a *radical* hope would be, we need to consider the existential situation of the Aboriginal Australian peoples. Our peoples have lost sovereignty over our lands, and the most numerous Aboriginal Australian peoples constitute less than 0.1 per cent of the population of the sovereign state where we are citizens. The continued existence of the Aboriginal Australian ethnicities is threatened by our status as unrecognised minorities in our own land, our apparent inability to maintain our Australian languages in the face of such adversity, and the extremity, numerically speaking, of our minority status.

Members of Anglophone peoples, such as the Non-Indigenous Australians, have difficulty understanding the existential angst of small ethnicities. It is easy to see why. The English language and the Anglophone culture are the most powerful forces in history. Anglophone culture is in a remarkable way intertwined with the growth of liberty, democracy and the rule of law, and its perpetual flourishing is therefore guaranteed. To become fluent in English is indeed an indispensable part of any child's education, anywhere in the world.

This blessing that Anglophone people have, that their culture will live because of its own momentum and its globally recognised value, is the opposite of the existential torment suffered by members of peoples such as the Guugu Yimidhirr people, to which I belong historically and linguistically, and through descent.

The Guugu Yimidhirr know that we have a language, a culture, a literature and a history – but the heritage of our part of the world is in danger of disappearing. Disappearing not only from the lives of people, but also by being incompletely recorded – and we Aboriginal Australians don't know how to stop it.

Where are the Livonians today? Where is the Barrow Point language?

I wrote that this existential angst is hard for Anglophone people to understand, but that is probably not correct. It may not be their own first thought when they consider the situation of Aboriginal Australians, but they understand when we explain it. One of Australia's most eminent business people wrote to me:

> What is also relevant here, Noel, is the idea you mentioned that in a democratic liberal tradition, the cultures which come out of Europe do not carry the burden of existential angst about heritage and culture. In other words, they have no fear of loss, even though their culture continues to evolve. On the other hand, Indigenous [Australian] people have a fear of loss of identity and culture – a fear well supported by 200 years of evidence. Understanding this fear is an expression of our common humanity.

The radical hope for Australia – for Indigenous Australians as well as Non-Indigenous Australians – is that the sovereign state of Australia becomes the recognised home of all native Australian ethnicities: the Guugu Yimidhirr, the Yolngu and the other Indigenous Australian peoples, and of the Non-Indigenous Australians.

The forms this recognition should take must be a debate for the whole country; a long journey which I can't even begin to discuss in this afterword. The only thing that must be said to make a discussion of radical hope meaningful is that language is critical – absolutely critical – and increasingly so.

I wrote that one of the best gifts for a child is absolute command of English and the Anglophone tradition. However, the greatest gift for a child in Australia – and it must be a gift from parents, community and government because it is too late to acquire it when we are old enough to choose our lives – is to have another language, a mother tongue, a language of the heart that is not English.

We all live surrounded by English in work and social life. The right of Australians is to have, from childhood, an inner voice that speaks another language and opens the gates to another world.

Why is this existentially necessary? For Australians to appreciate and answer that question, we need to acknowledge that the Anglophone culture may be history's greatest, but that there are some ideas that have been better comprehended by other cultures; the importance of multilingualism, and how multilingualism is preserved, is one of them.

The Swedes on the eastern shores of the Baltic Sea, for centuries separated from Sweden and for long periods under Russian or Soviet domination, said all that needs to be said in the title and in the first lines of their unofficial anthem:

The Song of the Mother Tongue
How sweetly the song resounds
In beloved mother tongue,
Consoling grief,
Honing the steel of the mind …

Feeling the threat of their minority culture's extinction, these Swedes picked the mother tongue as the sole theme of their anthem. They correctly observed that it is in your mother tongue that you have intellectual and spiritual freedom; minority languages must have a strong position for their traditional speakers to be truly free citizens in the sovereign states they share with majority peoples.

But, significantly, the first thing the anthem says is that the mother tongue consoles grief. All members of minorities understand why this is said first. There is much sorrow in human life; minorities face the additional grief of not being in charge of their people's destiny and the prospect of their cultural obliteration from history's page.

We Aboriginal Australians have lost most of our land, our sovereignty and most that once was ours. The necessary solace in this grief is to speak with my children in my ancestral and historical tongues. The necessary solace is to speak my Australian language, to read and sing the old texts from classical times and from the mission days that have been written down, and to build a living literature by writing more.

We do need economically and socially sustainable lives; but it is our cultural link with the past – a link which would break without language – that makes our lives spiritually sustainable as members of a conquered people. What we need more than anything else is to see that our tongues are not dying languages spoken only in a few homes, but languages with a future: growing, officially recognised languages of Australia.

Closing the gap is a necessary part of reconciliation. Land rights are also an essential part of the fulfilment of Stanner's hope that Indigenous Australians would be able to keep that which makes us who we are.

But we will have true reconciliation when millions of Australians speak our Australian languages from coast to coast. It is then that we will have the keys to our landscape, our history, our art, our stories. The Australian languages, and the literatures and cultures that live or have lived through them, are the most important things we have in Australia. Their revival, growth and use in all social, political, educational, commercial and cultural domains is the most important matter for Australia's future.

*

We have put so much effort into the Class domain in the Cape York Academy because without mainstream education, functional communities, strong families and economic integration, you can't do anything, let alone maintain culture. We have to make Class work, otherwise we have nothing to build on.

The Class domain is, however, largely off-the-shelf, albeit underpinned with a large amount of policy innovation (such as the Family Responsibilities Commission) to make sure the D.I. programs deliver to Cape York Peninsula communities what they have delivered to disadvantaged children in the United States.

It is with the next step, in the Culture domain, that we are attempting something truly new: the development of D.I.

programs in Australian languages. The scripted lessons that are currently being developed for the Hope Vale School are exclusively in the Guugu Yimdhirr language.

Education in Australian languages is not new; but teaching in Australian languages should not be done primarily because some children know too little English when they start school. It should also be done where children know more English, or predominantly or only English – this is the principle of the Culture domain in Cape York, where languages are dying.

Teaching children in Australian languages is only one instance of speaking to children in Australian languages so that they learn them as their mother tongues. If children do not learn Australian languages as mother tongues, Australian cultures cannot live.

If you don't know an Indigenous Australian language, learn one (people with no Indigenous Australian family may learn the language of the area with which they have the strongest ties). If you know an Indigenous Australian language, improve your grasp of it; literacy in Australian languages is still rare.

Then speak it to the children. This is the noblest and worthiest cause for an Australian patriot.

Noel Pearson
February 2011

Subscribe to Quarterly Essay
Receive a discount and never miss an issue. Mailed direct to your door.

....

☐ **1 year subscription** (4 issues): $49 a year within Australia incl. GST. Outside Australia $79.

☐ **2 year subscription** (8 issues): $95 a year within Australia incl. GST. Outside Australia $155.

* All prices include postage and handling.

....

Payment Details

☐ I enclose a cheque/money order made out to Schwartz Media Pty Ltd.

☐ Please debit my credit card (Mastercard, Visa or Bankcard accepted).

Card No. ☐☐☐☐ ☐☐☐☐ ☐☐☐☐ ☐☐☐☐

Expiry date   /   **Amount $**

Cardholder's name

Signature

Name

Address

Email

Post or Fax this form to:

Quarterly Essay, Reply Paid 79448, Melbourne, VIC 3000

Tel: (03) 9486 0288 / Fax: (03) 9486 0244

Email: subscribe@blackincbooks.com

Subscribe online: **www.quarterlyessay.com**

QUARTERLY ESSAY

Australia's best minds on the hottest topics.

Quarterly Essay presents significant contributions to the general debate. Each issue contains a single essay written at a length of about 25,000 words. It aims to present the widest range of political, intellectual and cultural opinion.

Subscribe online at **www.quarterlyessay.com**